No Greater LOVE

Other books by Karl Haffner

Caught Between Two Worlds
Soul Matters
Pilgrim's Problems
Out of the Hot Tub, Into the World
The Cure for Soul Fatigue

No
Greater
LOVE

"Greater love hath no man than this, that a man lay down his life for his friends." —JOHN 15:13

True Stories of the Ultimate Sacrifice

KARL HAFFNER

Pacific Press® Publishing Association
Nampa, Idaho
Oshawa, Ontario, Canada
www.pacificpress.com

Cover design by Gerald Lee Monks
Cover design resources from dreamstime.com and iStockphoto.com
Inside design by Kristin Hansen-Mellish

The author assumes full responsibility for the accuracy of all facts and quotations as cited in this book.

Unless otherwise indicated, all Scripture quotations are from the HOLY BIBLE, NEW INTERNATIONAL VERSION®, NIV®, copyright © 1973, 1978, 1984, 2011 by Biblica, Inc.™ Used by permission. All rights reserved worldwide.

Scripture quotations marked KJV are from the King James Version.

Scripture quotations from *The Message.* Copyright © by Eugene H. Peterson, 1993, 1994, 1995. Used by permission of NavPress Publishing Group.

Scripture quotations marked NCV are quoted from *The Holy Bible, New Century Version,* copyright © 1987, 1988, 1991 by Word Publishing, a division of Thomas Nelson, Inc. Used by permission.

Scripture quotations marked NKJV are from The New King James Version, copyright © 1979, 1980, 1982, Thomas Nelson, Inc., Publishers.

Scripture quotations marked NLT are taken from the Holy Bible, New Living Translation, copyright © 1996, 2004, 2007 by Tyndale House Foundation. Used by permission of Tyndale House Publishers Inc., Carol Stream, Illinois 60188. All rights reserved.

Scripture quotations marked TLB are from *The Living Bible,* copyright © 1971 by Tyndale House Publishers, Wheaton, IL. Used by permission.

You can obtain additional copies of this book by calling toll-free 1-800-765-6955 or by visiting www.adventistbookcenter.com.

Library of Congress Cataloging-in-Publication Data:

No greater love : true stories of the ultimate sacrifice / compiled and written by Karl Haffner.
    p. cm.
 ISBN 13: 978-0-8163-3789-7 (pbk.)
 ISBN 10: 0-8163-3789-6 (pbk.)
 1. Sacrifice—Christianity. 2. Love—Religious aspects—Christianity.
3. Seventh-day Adventists—Doctrines. I. Haffner, Karl, 1961-
 BV4509.5.N6 2012
 242—dc23
                              2012029555

12 13 14 15 16 • 5 4 3 2 1

Dedication

To my dad, Pastor Cliff Haffner,
who not only told many of these cherished stories but lived them.
Dad, your life has been a consistent and convincing
sermon of sacrifice, grace, and love.
There is no man on earth that I respect more than you.

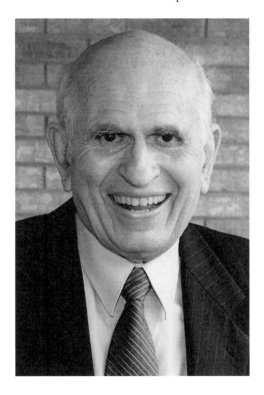

Acknowledgments

Dawn Noorbergen Surridge, Violet L. M. Curtis Prouty, Father Edward Schmidt, Mark and Wendy Witas, Lynne Hughes and Anthea Collett, Carl and Carol Cosaert, Darold and Barbara Bigger, Moody Adams, and Doug Sterner for generously sharing your stories. Without you, there is no book.

Joe Wheeler for warning me that anthologies are not for the faint of heart (were you ever prophetic on that one), but patiently coaching me through the land mines.

Jerry Thomas, Scott Cady, Tim Lale, and the entire crew at Pacific Press® for your tireless work in getting this project launched after thirteen years.

Everyone on the Kettering pastoral team for graciously covering my duties during a sabbatical.

Cheryl Haffner for sharing Dad's picture.

Cherié, Lindsey, and Claire for the smiles you put on my face everyday.

Contents

Dad's Communion File

I'LL NEVER FORGET THE STORY YOUR FATHER TOLD ONE COMMUNION SABBATH," Mr. Carpenter reflected. "Even though it's been twenty-five years since I was the head elder and he was the pastor here, I still remember it. I haven't heard the story since, but it was about a girl in North Dakota who was caught in a blizzard. As I recall, her name was Hazel Miner." Mr. Carpenter guided me through the touching details of a story that I, too, had heard my father tell.

Mr. Carpenter recounted the sobering sacrifice that Hazel Miner made to rescue her siblings. His voice cracked while his eyes leaked. Tears sopped his well-defined wrinkles as he connected the story to the sacrifice of Christ—just as my father had done decades before.

I zoomed in for a close-up shot. I wanted to spotlight the moment on video to show at my dad's surprise retirement party. In that profound and holy exchange, I sensed Mr. Carpenter whispering my father's legacy. This tribute of memorable stories was echoed by parishioners who spanned forty-three years of ministry and accented five hours of video interviews. The common thread that wove through the tapestry of memories was this predictable comment: "Every quarter for the Communion service, your dad would tell a story. I loved those stories."

I, too, remember those church services with special fondness. I hated to miss Communion Sabbath—not because I was some superspiritual kid; actually it was because we got out of church early and I liked that. Fifteen minutes was all Dad needed to take us to Calvary through a story of human sacrifice. No preaching, little moralizing—the story was all we'd get that week. But those stories remain long after most sermons are forgotten.

Today, those sermons (along with other stories that I have found) are stuffed into a fat file that I labeled "Dad's Communion Stories." As a pastor, I retrieve that file every quarter to hunt for a story to share at a Communion service. The tales trigger vibrant memories of sitting in a pew, hanging on my father's every word. Some stories take me back to the Providence Seventh-day Adventist Church, where my dad baptized me. Other stories remind me of the embarrassment I felt as a teenager in the Roanoke Seventh-day Adventist Church, watching my dad sob through a story. Still other stories spark memories of impactful collisions with the Cross as I grappled to comprehend the scandalous nature of God's love and His atonement.

Dad's Communion stories shaped my soul unlike any seminary course in Greek or homiletics or eschatology. Even the stories that have now blurred with age are for me clearer snapshots of grace than any heady lecture I regurgitated on an essay exam. Such is the power of story.

"It would be well," Ellen G. White tells us, "to spend a thoughtful hour each day reviewing the life of Christ from the manger to Calvary. We should take it point by point and let the imagination vividly grasp each scene, especially the closing ones of His earthly life."[1] It has been my experience that no other spiritual practice has as equal an impact as lingering in the shadow of the Cross for an hour each day. This book offers a companion guide as you go to Calvary. My prayer is that you will see God's sacrifice in a fresh way, through new eyes.

Years ago, I attended the Passion play in Puyallup, Washington. Scores of folk had talked it up, and for years, I had intended to go. Then someone told me that local pastors got free admission. OK, that got me there.

At dusk, we settled into our seats just behind the sound board, which I swear covered an acre. Sound and light technicians danced about, busily tweaking hundreds of knobs and sliders.

Wow! I thought as the drama unfolded. *This production rivals Hollywood.* There were hundreds of actors. Camels, horses, sheep, and goats provided the feel of first-century Palestine. And then came the special effects: thunder, lightning, walking on water.

Sitting next to me was a woman who obviously didn't know the story. While I am quick to claim eavesdropping as my primary spiritual gift, in this setting, I found her interruptions to be annoying.

"Who is that man?" she asked the guy next to her.

"Oh, um, that's Peter."

"Who was Peter?"

"Well," he stammered, "Peter was one of Jesus' disciples."

"Disciples?"

"Yea, disciples, um, well, see, Jesus ran with this gang of twelve guys. But they weren't called the Crips or the Bloods—well, maybe they would have called themselves the Bloods." He was clearly amused by his double entendre that flew right over her head. "Anyway, His gang—they were called disciples."

"Oh, *cooooool,*" she sighed, her curiosity quieted for a few ticks.

"Holy Moses! Did Jesus really make that blind man see, or was it mostly smoke and mirrors?"

"He really was a Miracle Worker," her friend explained.

Meanwhile, I sat there coveting. *I wish we could pull off half this stuff for our annual Christmas pageant. I wonder where they get their camels. And how do they get angels that look so authentic? I love those uniforms on the Roman soldiers. The dramas at our church are painfully lame.*

The special effects got cranked up to a whole new level when they hoisted Jesus on the cross. Lightning lit up the sky. Thunder rumbled our seats. The violence against Jesus made me grimace. I couldn't watch.

The woman next to me was equally shaken. Tugging the arm of her friend, she demanded, "Why are they killing Him? What are they doing? He never did nothing bad to them."

"You're right," he said. "But you see, this was God's only way to restore a broken relationship with the rebellious human race. God will not tolerate sin. The 'wages of sin is death,' the Bible says. So, when we sin, we should die. But, instead, God sent His Son to take our punishment."

With that simple gospel presentation, she came undone. She convulsed with long, jagged sobs.

Not until Jesus exploded out of the tomb did her crying stop. As if to confirm that she was not imagining the good news, she asked, "Wait a minute! He came back to life? Jesus died and then came back to life?"

"It's true," the man confirmed.

With that, she jumped to her feet and shouted, *"Un-be-liev-able!"* Turning to me now, she wanted to make sure I didn't miss the best part of the play. "Check that out," she squealed. "He's alive again. He must have been God! He came back from the dead!"

Of course, I was quite versed in the story. I'm ashamed to admit that rather than being undone by the gospel story, I was infatuated with the lighting, lightning, acting, sound—the whole experience was breathtaking. I'm embarrassed to tell you that I have handled the story so much—preached it, studied it, explained it—that it no longer affected me as it did that woman.

God forgive me, I prayed as I shuffled out of the amphitheater. *I have become calloused to the greatest story ever told. Rekindle my spirit and soften my heart by Your grace.*

It is my prayer that these stories will awaken something deep inside you that tugs your soul toward a fresh and invigorating picture of Calvary. These stories capture amazing acts of courage—many of them heroic decisions to die so others might live.

In his book *Lone Survivor,* Marcus Luttrell shares one such story when he and a couple of other United States Navy SEALs battled a heavily armed force of Taliban soldiers in the mountains of Afghanistan. He would be the lone survivor, thanks to a decision made by his comrade, Lieutenant Michael Patrick Murphy.

Amid a firestorm of bullets, Murphy bravely marched into a clearing on the battlefield that day—the only place where he could get cell-phone reception and call for backup. Luttrell describes Murphy's decision: "His objective was clear: to make one last valiant attempt to save his two teammates. He made the call, made the connection. He reported our approximate position, the strength of our enemy, and how serious the situation was."[2]

As expected, the enemy shot Murphy. It was, in Luttrell's words, "An act of supreme valor." He says, "Lieutenant Mikey was a wonderful person and a very, very great SEAL officer. If they build a memorial to him as high as the Empire State Building, it won't ever be high enough for me."[3]

Indeed, any memorial to someone who makes such a sacrifice seems pitifully insufficient. No memorial, no book, no building, no medal of honor, no song, no story can adequately honor such love.

So I recognize at the outset of our journey to Calvary together that these stories do not fully capture the essence of the Cross—the supreme memorial of love. Ellen G. White tells us, "The cross of Christ will be the science and the song of the redeemed through all eternity. In Christ glorified they will behold Christ crucified."[4] Indeed, eternity begs for time to comprehend the Cross.

While these stories dimly illuminate the Cross, any insight into the sacrifice of Jesus is worthy of our attention. Perhaps your experience will be similar to mine, and you will remember the stories. In passing along the symbols of the Last Supper, Jesus said, "Do this in remembrance of me."[5]

So visit the Cross and remember. Remember the blood. Remember the broken body. Remember the death. And rejoice in God's undying love.

·❧·

His Broken Body

He himself bore our sins in his body on the tree.
—1 Peter 2:24

Uncle Harold's Love Story

by Robert Surridge

W*HY WOULD JESUS GO THROUGH WITH IT?*
Tormentors "spit in Jesus' face and beat him with their fists. And some slapped him, jeering, 'Prophesy to us, you Messiah! Who hit you that time?' " (Matthew 26:67, 68, NLT).

"They stripped him and put a scarlet robe on him. They wove thorn branches into a crown and put it on his head, and they placed a reed stick in his right hand as a scepter. Then they knelt before him in mockery and taunted, 'Hail! King of the Jews!' And they spit on him and grabbed the stick and struck him on the head with it. When they were finally tired of mocking him, they took off the robe and put his own clothes on him again. Then they led him away to be crucified" (Matthew 27:28–32, NLT).

Why would Jesus willingly subject Himself to such inhumane torture? What kept Him pinned to the tree? It wasn't the spikes. Nor was it the Roman soldiers.

It was love—pure and simple.

Jesus determined to cling to that cross for the sake of His family—you and me. Naked, bleeding, mangled, and thrashed, He would not let go. There was no limit to where Jesus would go in order to reconcile the lost human race to His Father.

Why?

One reason: love.

One thing I regret is not having met some of my grandparents' brothers and sisters who died before I was born. My grandmother comes from Nottingham-shire in England, and most of the men in her family were coal miners. Many of them hardly lived long enough for my father, let alone me, to know them. Some were killed in accidents down in the mine. Others coughed themselves to an early grave from miners' lung.

The one I really regret not having met, though he died only a few years ago, was my great-uncle Harold. Harold Gascoigne was a Nottinghamshire miner—like his brother, cousin, father, and grandfather. He was a big, strong man, but gentle, soft-spoken, and dependable.

Harold took pride in his job, though it was often mundane, dirty, and dangerous. It's probably done by a machine nowadays. But Harold worked on the floor of the mine loading the lift cage with full coal tubs. Once the cage was full, it would be cranked by a winch hundreds of feet to the surface.

Harold's job had to be done quickly and efficiently. Each trip to the top cost money and time. If the cage wasn't full, coal would bottleneck at the bottom, and a shortage would develop at the top. If Harold took too long maneuvering the filled coal tubs into the cage, the number of trips up and down the shaft in a day would be reduced.

There was also safety to consider. The coal tubs had to fit securely in the lift cage. If one were to start rolling about during the trip to the surface, the whole lift shaft assembly could become unbalanced and damaged. The sliding gates of the cage were also Harold's responsibility. If they weren't secure, well . . . the results didn't bear thinking about.

In a job like Harold's, one day was very much like the next. The only thing that seemed to indicate the passing of months and years was wear and tear on the equipment. Harold noticed one thing in particular. One of the bashed, dented, and battered coal tubs, through use, now no longer fit snugly in the cage. This caused difficulty in sending a full load. But Uncle Harold was conscientious and did his best to overcome problems caused by the deteriorating equipment.

On one particular shift, though, everything began to go wrong. It had been a hard day. The pit ponies that dragged wagons full of coal tubs to the lift cap had been acting up, the coal dust seemed more choking and blinding than usual, and the coal tubs, heavier and more awkward. Harold had just closed the cage gates on another load when he saw that one tub was dangerously askew.

The warning bell for the pull to begin sounded. Quickly he reached over the top of the lift gate to give the tub a sharp jolt into place. Harold knew the timing of the warning bell and had rightly judged that he had a few seconds to get back to safety. What he hadn't judged correctly was that someone would send the message to go ahead and winch the cage up before the warning period ended and without visually checking the cage area.

A thousand feet above, the winching gear slammed suddenly into action, and the cage jerked up into the shaft. Harold, still bent over it, went with it.

The first thing he felt was a beam, and then crosspieces of the shaft smashing into his legs and lower back. As the shaft narrowed, these blows dragged him backward and down along the side of the cage. But he held on like grim death. His left hand managed to grab on to a part of the cage, and that, along with tangled clothing wrapped in the bars, stopped him from being dragged out completely.

The cage stopped.

It was more than a quarter of the way up. Harold's shocked workmates had finally managed to get a message to the top ordering them to stop the lift cage.

But what now? Harold was beyond reach. The operator tried to reverse the cage, but it seemed stuck. Slowly the miners realized that Harold's body must be jamming the cage.

The team leader below shone a powerful torch beam up the shaft. He could barely see the cage and Harold's body hanging off one side. The miners gasped. He must be dead.

"Silence!" the leader demanded.

They heard a moan.

"Harold?"

Another moan.

The team leader knew that Harold had to be desperately injured, and that the rest of the trip would probably kill him. But even though it was farther up than down, Harold would have to go to the surface eventually to get proper medical attention. The leader made a decision. The best thing was to get him up now—no matter what state he was in.

They passed the message up the phone to the surface. "Proceed, dead slow!" The miners at the bottom heard the cage jerk upward. A moment later something fell at their feet. It was a thumb.

The cage went up at the slowest pace possible, but there was still not enough room between the shaft wall and the cage for Harold's body. His back, legs, and limp right arm were gradually scraped raw by each beam. It was somewhere on that agonizing journey that Harold lost two more fingers from his right hand. The pain was agonizing. And the cage seemed to be actively trying to shake him loose, while the shaft wall tried to snatch him off and drag him down.

But it was something very specific that gave Harold the ability to cling to the cage as it dragged him upward. Dreadful, heartbreaking pictures flashed through Harold's mind. He kept seeing the face of his wife, Beatrix, and his young son, Trevor. First as the news of his death reached them, then at his graveside, then being evicted from their home, his wife a widow and his son an orphan. He couldn't, he *wouldn't,* let that happen.

His family needed him; they were more important than the pain, the weariness, and the fear. He loved his wife and son passionately. He had to see them again.

It would have been such a relief to let go. It would have been so easy, but his family was everything to him. For them he would endure, for them he would hang on, for them he would take the pain and punishment no matter how long it took.

When the cage reached the surface, a half hour after it started its terrible journey, Harold was barely conscious. He was almost naked, his clothes torn away by the shaft wall. His right arm was smashed and twisted double, both his legs and hips were broken, and he had lost two fingers and the thumb from his right hand.

But his left hand was locked solid to the lift cage, and it took two burly miners to pry it free. Harold had hung on; he had not let go. It was the power of love and the true grit of family loyalty that had given him the strength to cling to that cage. For the sake of his family he had held on.[1]

A Glimpse of Heaven's Hero

A LOCAL WINDSHIELD REPAIR COMPANY HAS LAUNCHED A MARKETING BLITZ *on the radio that highlights stories of Congressional Medal of Honor recipients. Because commuting gobbles up a chunk of my day, on many occasions I have enjoyed a thirty-second respite from ESPN sports chatter to hear the story of a brave warrior who made the ultimate sacrifice.*

Jason Dunham is the hero of one such story. The commercial about him prompted me to research this brave man who gave his life in the line of duty. I salute Jason and the many other brave men and women who selflessly defend my freedoms. In their heroism, we catch a glimpse of heaven's Hero.

If you Google Scio [*sigh-oh*], you'll get the basic facts about a sleepy town of 1,833 tucked away in southwestern New York. The settlement began in 1805 with Joseph Knight, a minuteman in the American Revolution. Spanning the town's two centuries of history, *Wikipedia* lists only one person—Jason Dunham—under the heading of "Notable Residents."[1]

Jason was born on November 10, 1981, to Natalie Walker, a sixteen-year-old mother, and a father who didn't stick around to introduce himself. When Jason was eight months old, his mother married Dan Dunham, an employee at a local dairy farm, but that relationship soon fell apart as well. Dan adopted Jason; and along with his new wife, Deb, he raised Jason and his three siblings—two brothers and a sister. "We told Jason from the beginning that he was adopted," says Deb Dunham, a home-economics teacher. "It didn't matter, I consider him my son, and we're all one family. I remember when he was about 6 or so, he would hug me and say, 'You can be my mother.' "[2]

A standout in sports at Scio Central High School, "Jason excelled in soccer, basketball and baseball. He received All Allegany County League honors in basketball and baseball."[3]

Upon graduation in 2000, Jason enlisted in the United States Marine Corps, earning the rank of corporal. Standing six feet one inch tall, with a muscular build and hazel eyes, he was a Marine's Marine and a born leader.

A friend described Jason as " 'a good old country boy' who liked to play pool, flirt and listen to Tim McGraw CDs." "He was the toughest Marine but the nicest guy. He would do anything for you. Cpl. Dunham was the kind of person everybody wants as their best friend."[4]

Jason's men loved and respected him at least in part because Jason treated every person—especially the underdog—with respect. Reflecting on the cruel pranks and initiation rites that many new recruits endured, Jason wrote, "Through my experiences in the Marine Corps, the one thing that stands out more than anything else is the fact that Marines abuse their power. . . . [F]or some reason they have the need to make and watch other Marines do pointless and senseless things. . . . Watching them sweat and become fatigued is considered good fun for most marines."[5] For Jason, bullying the "boots," as they were called, was neither good nor fun.

Following a stint as a security force sentry at the Naval Submarine Base Kings Bay in Georgia from 2000 to 2003, Jason was transferred to Camp Husaybah, a high-elevation outpost near the Syrian border. There he served as squad leader in Kilo Company's Fourth Platoon.

In March 2004, Jason joined a spirited debate among his comrades that questioned the best way to deal with an incoming hand grenade. The Marine Corps manuals spell out what to do in almost every situation in warfare. In the event of dealing with a live grenade, however, the handbooks offer no formal instructions. "Second Lt. Brian 'Bull' Robinson suggested that if a marine lay face down on the grenade and held it between his forearms, the ceramic bulletproof plate in his flak vest might be strong enough to protect his vital organs. His arms would shatter, but he might live."[6]

Jason argued that a marine's Kevlar helmet covering the grenade might soften the explosion enough for the marine to survive. A few weeks later, these men would clearly remember the details of the discussion.

On April 14, 2004, three days after Easter Sunday, Corporal Dunham was leading a fourteen-man foot patrol when a report came in about a roadside bomb hitting some nearby marines. Racing to the scene, Corporal Dunham's patrol split into two teams to search for the insurgents. Shortly after noon, Corporal Dunham's team approached a line of seven Iraqi vehicles parked in an alleyway.

As the marines searched the vehicles, the driver of a beat-up Land Cruiser bounded out and attacked Corporal Dunham. Reacting to the skirmish, two colleagues raced to assist, but Dunham yelled, "No, no, no—watch his hand!"[7]

Staff Sergeant John Ferguson, then thirty, of Aurora, Colorado, "who heard Dunham's last words before the grenade blast, saw the insurgent and the three Marines sprawled" in the dirt.

" 'I thought for sure all four were dead,' he said. Amazingly, though, Lance

Cpl. William Hampton and Pfc. Kelly Miller . . . rose to their feet. Dunham never regained consciousness."[8]

In the insurgent's hand had been a Mills bomb hand grenade that rolled loose—the pin already pulled. Corporal Dunham reacted instantaneously by putting his theory on how to react to a live grenade to the test. Throwing his Kevlar helmet on the grenade, he covered it with his body to protect his squad members from the blast. The explosion left Corporal Dunham unconscious, lying face down in a pool of his own blood.

"I deeply believe that given the facts and evidence presented he clearly understood the situation and attempted to block the blast," said the then forty-year-old Lieutenant Colonel Matthew Lopez of Chicago. "His personal action was far beyond the call of duty and saved the lives of his fellow Marines."[9]

With serious shrapnel wounds to the head, Corporal Dunham was transported to Baghdad, then to Germany, and finally to the National Naval Medical Center in Bethesda, Maryland, where his parents, Dan and Deb Dunham, met him.

"Jason's condition is very, very grim," the doctor explained. "I have to tell you the outlook isn't very promising." The shrapnel had traveled down the side of his brain, causing irreversible damage. Blood in the urine suggested kidney failure. One lung had collapsed, and the other was filling with fluid.[10] Eight days after the incident, on April 22, 2004, at 4:43 P.M., Marine Corporal Jason Lee Dunham died. "Six days later, Third Battalion gathered in the parking lot outside the al Qa'im command post for psalms and ceremony. In a traditional combat memorial, one Marine plunged a rifle, bayonet-first, into a sandbag. Another placed a pair of tan combat boots in front, and a third perched a helmet on the rifle's stock."[11]

Back home in New York, numerous memorials commemorate Jason's heroic sacrifice. In Scio, a stretch of State Route 19, a bridge that crosses Interstate 86, and a local post office all carry his name. At one ceremony, Assemblyman Daniel Burling said, "Corporal Jason Dunham is a true American hero who faithfully served his country and led by example."[12]

On January 11, 2007, President George W. Bush posthumously presented Corporal Dunham with the Congressional Medal of Honor. This recognition came at the prompting of New York Democrat Senator Charles Schumer. In a letter to the president, Schumer wrote, " 'Corporal Dunham unflinchingly gave what Lincoln deemed "the last full measure of devotion" and his heroism reflects the true spirit of selflessness, leadership, and courage that the Medal of Honor was established to recognize. . . . Corporal Dunham lay down his life by shielding members of his unit from danger by throwing himself on a live grenade, an act of unbelievable bravery and selflessness that saved the lives of at least two fellow Marines.' " At the ceremony, President Bush heralded Corporal Dunham for his selflessness in giving "his own life so that the men under his command might live."[13]

On March 20, 2007, Corporal Dunham received still another monumental tribute when the navy announced that a new *Arleigh Burke*–class guided missile destroyer would be named the USS *Jason Dunham* in order to preserve the story of this American hero.[14] The keynote speaker at the warship's commissioning ceremony, Marine Corps Commandant General Jim Amos, posted in an e-mail to *Marine Corps Times* that "Corporal Jason Dunham and the Dunham family epitomize the word selflessness. A true hero, Jason's selfless act of heroism and leadership . . . will never be forgotten."[15]

In Jason, we find a glimpse of Jesus.

Dai Hankey reminds us that

Jesus was the hero of heaven who had came to save us from the curse of sin, but rather than coming as a mighty warrior, or a charismatic political leader, He came as a vulnerable baby, dependent on a mother for food and warmth. He embraced the fullness of humanity from the cradle to the grave, knowing like us, what it means to grow up in a painful, broken world, to face every trial and feel every emotion. He laughed, He cried, He triumphed and He trembled.

He knows what true life feels like from our perspective, which is awesome because it reveals to us that God is not a loveless, distant God who doesn't give a stuff about what we go through. Rather, He is a good God who is willing to step right to the heart of where we are at in order to reveal His love to us.[16]

"We do not have a high priest who is unable to empathize with our weaknesses, but we have one who has been tempted in every way, just as we are—yet he did not sin. Let us then approach God's throne of grace with confidence, so that we may receive mercy and find grace to help us in our time of need" (Hebrews 4:15, 16).

Greater Love

By Violet L. M. Curtis

D AD TOLD THE STORY ABOUT NAT AND PETER WELL—AND OFTEN. BUT THE *only documentation of the story came from cryptic notes that he had compiled from a source he couldn't remember. I, too, have told this story often—but always with a smoldering frustration that its source was unverified.*

With the advent of Google, I assumed that tracking down this story would be possible. On numerous occasions through the years, however, I had tried every imaginable combination of key word searches for its source—all without success. So it was with steeped skepticism that I attempted a last-ditch effort to find the story just before sending this manuscript to the editors for publication. On my this-really-really-really-is-my-last-Google-search-for-this-story attempt, I got a hit from a Web site posting Seventh-day Adventist archived publications. Turns out, it was published in The Youth's Instructor *during World War II.*

After a little more detective work, I contacted the author, Violet L. M. Curtis Prouty, who shared helpful information about this story. She told me that originally it was written for a class assignment—with no intention of publication. While the story has some factual elements based on stories she remembers from her upbringing in Newfoundland, it should really be classified as fiction. I include it in this collection, however, because it illustrates a historical fact—that Jesus willingly died even for His enemies.

For years Peter had been Nat's enemy—ever since Nat had thrashed him for torturing a cat. Peter vowed revenge, and as they grew up together, tried in many ways to get even with Nat.

Both boys lived in a little fishing village on the wave-washed shores of New-foundland. As they grew into young manhood, both chose fishing as their occupation. Keen competition was displayed, for neither cared to have the other known as a better fisherman.

Then one day a comely, witty young woman named Anne, and her parents, came to live in this village. Her father was a fisherman too. Nat and Peter became friendly with her and were once again competitors—this time for the young woman's affections. Anne liked both of them; for a time it was a question as to which she would choose. Anxious hours both Nat and Peter spent until finally Anne made her choice. Nat was the favored suitor. Again Peter was incensed against Nat and renewed his vow of revenge. But the happy bride and groom knew nothing of the fire of hatred that was burning within Peter's breast.

The night of the wedding a large new moon shed a radiant luster over the little fishing hamlet and the great ocean that washed its shores. The little white church on the hill was crowded with people all eager to see the happy couple united in marriage. But Peter was not there. On a rocky shelf overlooking the peaceful, moonlit sea he stood and vowed that he would get even with Nat.

The newlyweds spent several days holidaying, and then settled in a pretty little vine-covered cottage near the beach. Peter went to sea.

Several years passed, and then a curly-haired boy came to gladden his parents' hearts. Nat spent all his spare moments with the young Nat, "the li'l shaver," as they called him. Sometimes Nat would tell him stories of the sea, but Anne did not like his tales. Often she would shake her head in disapproval, but little Nat always clamored for more. As he grew up, he became possessed of a deep longing to sail across the ocean and see some of the world. Often when the weather was not stormy, he accompanied his father to the fishing grounds. At these times he would sit dreamy-eyed in the bow of the boat, looking away across the water, longing with all the fervor of his passionate soul to sail afar.

As Anne would stand in the door of the cottage waving goodbye to her "two men," she would wonder how she could draw the curly-haired little lad's interest from distant lands. But always when he returned, he was more enthusiastic than ever to sail on the sea's broad bosom. At night as he lay in his bed, he would listen to the waves washing over the stones and singing a sweet lullaby. Or sometimes he would hear great reefers break in upon the rocks. Always the sea lured him.

He completed his education in the village school and turned to helping his father at fishing; yet his parents knew that his heart was out on the great sea. One day he came to Anne and said, "Mother, I must go. Please give me your permission." She, looking down into his eyes, saw love and affection written there, as well as burning desire.

"Yes, Nat, you may go," she answered, trying to speak calmly.

"Thank you, Mother," he said, and enveloped her in his strong, young arms.

It was a sad day when he left. Even the wind, as it moaned through the leaves, seemed sorry. But with brave smiles and tearful eyes, Anne and Nat said goodbye to "the li'l shaver." Young Nat, on reaching the large seaport two hundred miles from his home, signed on a vessel bound for England.

After several days at sea, he wondered why he was getting all the hard and unpleasant tasks, for he was sure that he was not the only "greenhorn" on board. Then he discovered that the captain was none other than Peter, the old enemy and one-time rival of his father. And Peter was working out his revenge! During the voyage, he seemed to vent all his spite on the boy. He worked him so hard, spoke to him so very harshly, and made his life so miserable that young Nat decided he would "sign off" when he got back to port again.

On the return voyage, the boat ran into a fierce storm, such as only the Atlantic Ocean knows. Thunder roared, rain poured down in a steady sheet, fog enveloped them, and huge whitecaps beat at the ship's side. Nat, who was working on deck, was washed overboard. The fierceness of the storm would not permit a rescue; so the boat plowed on without him.

When the ship arrived in port, one of his shipmates went to Anne and Nat Senior and told the story, adding, "He didn't need to be on deck, but the captain, who for some reason didn't like him, said he must stay around and help out."

Anne, crushed by the blow, fell ill. Nat felt a great hatred for Peter spring up in his heart, but he tried to conceal it from Anne. Two days and nights he stayed by her side as she went down into the valley of the shadow of death. Those days were filled with heartache as he saw his beloved slip from him. The hatred he held for Peter grew. After days of suffering, Anne whispered goodbye and was gone from his life forever.

Nat was left alone to think over the happy days when he and Anne and "the li'l shaver" were all together in the little home. Somehow hatred could not abide with thoughts of those happy days; yet that happy home was broken because of one man. Many and varied were his feelings. Sometimes he could forgive and forget Peter, and then a sense of his loss would rush over him, and he would feel the old hate again. *It is not right that I should hate so,* he thought. Fervently he prayed that he might overcome the bitterness in his heart; yet often it came over him, and he felt himself unable to cope with it.

And then the storm came! The furious wind lashed the waves into strands and cast them into the air with a deafening roar. Sleet and snow filled the atmosphere, veiling the face of the sun from the fury of the elements. On into the night the storm continued. Many hearts sent up prayers of earnest entreaty through the long, dark hours for those in peril on the sea.

At daybreak the anxious fishermen peered through their windows out toward the wild, tossing ocean. A cry went up in every home. "A boat! Shipwreck!" the men dashed into their oilskins. Soon a group of hardy seamen were endeavoring to launch a boat, but the wind, hooting in derision, tore it from them, and the huge billows quickly demolished it. In sorrow they returned to their homes to pray for a lull in the tempest.

Two hours passed. At last two boats were launched. Nat jumped into one. Pulling heavily in the swell of the sea against the furious waves, the men reached the doomed ship. Then began the dangerous and arduous task of getting the crew into the boats before the ship sank forever into the boiling waters. One boat was filled and pushed off toward shore. Nat's boat was left to take off the remainder of the crew.

The struggle against the vicious sea continued. Finally the deck was cleared and the rescue boat could hold no more.

"Pull aft!" shouted Nat.

"Wait! The skipper is sick down below," shouted the fireman.

"Then pull for'ard," yelled Nat, as he prepared to leave the rescue boat. The craft pulled alongside; he leaped aboard and made for the captain's cabin.

"Hello!" he shouted.

"Yes," came a faint reply, "I'm here on the bunk."

Tenderly Nat lifted the sick man into his arms and hastened through the door. Once there, he stopped short, for in the gray light he recognized the face of Peter. A tide of feelings surged over him. Again he saw his wife suffer and die because of Peter's cruelty to "the li'l shaver." Hatred, black hatred, was in his eyes. Now he would be revenged. Then his eyes softened, and he hurried toward the waiting boat, bearing the heavy form of the captain.

"Easy now, men," he commanded, as the sailors lifted the sick captain into the boat. "All right? Pull away!"

"Oh, no, Nat. There's room for you here," they urged.

"No," Nat answered, "the boat'll sink with a pound more weight. Pull away!"

It was useless to argue, and to delay was disastrous, for the ship was fast settling on its starboard side. With heavy hearts and unwilling hands the sailors pulled away. They had gone only a few hundred yards when the ship settled for its final plunge and quietly slipped off the rock into the icy depths, bearing Nat with it.

Several days later the captain recovered from the shock and exposure to discover that it was Nat who had given his life to save him. Tears rolled down his rough cheeks, and he bowed his head in shame. "Forgive, O Lord," he prayed, "even as he forgave."

In the village graveyard beside Anne's grave, Peter placed a stone bearing the inscription:

"NAT MERCER
'Greater love hath no man than this.'
He laid down his life for an enemy."[1]

"I Loved and I Followed Christ"

By Father Edward Schmidt, SJ

A LITTLE DIGGING ON THE INTERNET UNCOVERED THIS TOUCHING STORY OF A *missionary who loved an unlovable teen, much as Jesus loves us. In the end, I believe Richie got his wish to be remembered as one who loved and followed Christ—even to his death.*

Richie Fernando was a long way from home. He was a Filipino Jesuit in Buddhist Cambodia. He was educated and full of promise in a camp where refugees maimed by bullets and land mines and scarred by hunger and disease fought for hope. He loved life in a land where life was hard and death nearby.

Richie went to Cambodia in May 1995 as part of his Jesuit training. He had entered the Society in 1990 and finished the novitiate and collegiate studies. Before going on to theology studies and ordination, he was sent to work at Banteay Prieb, a Jesuit technical school for the handicapped not far from Phnom Penh. Banteay Prieb describes itself as a "place that enables the disabled to tell their own stories, to gather strength and hope from being with one another, and to learn a new skill that enhances a sense of dignity and worth." Here people disabled by land mines, polio, and accidents learn skills that allow them to earn a living. Banteay Prieb means "the Center of the Dove."

When Richie arrived, his devotion to the students quickly won their trust. He began learning their Khmer language and came to appreciate their religious traditions. And he loved to share their stories, stories of survival during Pol Pot's genocidal regime, stories of the devastation of their society through poverty, displacement, and the nine million land mines that still plague their land.

One of these survivors is Sarom. Already an orphan, at sixteen Sarom became a soldier; two years later he was maimed by a land mine. Sarom finished his courses at Banteay Prieb and wanted to stay on there, but school authorities found him disruptive and asked him to leave. Richie Fernando mentioned Sarom in a letter to his friends in the Philippines, saying that although Sarom was "tricky," he still had a place in Richie's heart.

On October 17, 1996, Sarom came to the school for a meeting. Angered, he suddenly reached into a bag he was carrying, pulled out a grenade, and began to move toward a classroom full of students; the windows of the room were barred, leaving the students no escape. Richie Fernando came up behind Sarom and grabbed him.

"Let me go, teacher; I do not want to kill you," Sarom pleaded. But he dropped his grenade, and it fell behind him and Richie. In a flash Richie Fernando was dead, falling over with Sarom still grasped in his arms, protecting him from the violence he had made.

Only four days before his death, Richie had written a long letter to his friend Totet Banaynal. "I know where my heart is," he wrote; "It is with Jesus Christ, who gave his all for the poor, the sick, the orphan. . . . I am confident that God never forgets his people: our disabled brothers and sisters. And I am glad that God has been using me to make sure that our brothers and sisters know this fact. I am convinced that this is my vocation."

Three days after Richie's death, his shocked family and friends in the Philippines celebrated his funeral. At the same time, his shocked Cambodian friends carried an urn containing cloths soaked in his blood to a Buddhist funeral mound. In their shock they mourned; and in their mourning they gave thanks for Richie, the man they knew and loved, their son, their brother, their teacher, their friend.

Shocked by what he had caused, Sarom sat in his jail cell and mourned too. In March 1997, Richie's parents, Mr. and Mrs. Fernando, wrote to Cambodia's King Sihanouk, asking for pardon for Sarom; somehow, someone had to stop the violence. Sarom had not wanted to kill Richie. "Richie ate rice with me," he said. "He was my friend."

Days before his death, Richie confided in his diary: "I wish, when I die, people remember not how great, powerful, or talented I was, but that I served and spoke for the truth, I gave witness to what is right, I was sincere in all my works and actions. In other words, I loved and I followed Christ. Amen."[1]

A *Brady Bunch* of Love

G‍ROWING UP IN A FAMILY OF FOUR KIDS, I LEARNED THAT EVERY DAY WAS *crazy. Pranks, squabbles, sickness, and all sorts of tomfoolery shaped life as we knew it. Perhaps the similarity of sibling conflict helped to explain why this story carved a deep impression in me when Dad shared it for a Communion service. As a kid, I marveled that one child's life could be spared by another child's death.*

Sibling rivalry is as old as the Bible (Ishmael and Isaac, Jacob and Esau, Joseph and his brothers, and so on); but so is sibling love. Deep within the human heart lies untarnished bonds of love shared only between brothers and sisters. This story opens a window that helps us glimpse sibling love, thus illuminating our Father's love toward us.

For Edward and Dedi Taylor, six kids weren't enough. When the news of another child hit this family from Sparta, New Jersey, nine-year-old Ned excitedly prepared for the arrival of "my baby brother."

Jacqui was born in August 1964. *"Ooooh nooo!"* whined Ned. "I don't want another sister!"

When Edward shared Ned's reaction with Dedi, she scribbled a note:

"Dear Ned,

"I know you're disappointed, but of course it was never up to us to decide the girl-boy bit. It was always in God's hands. So please try to think instead of how very lucky we are to have a healthy, normal baby. And since you are the oldest of the boys, maybe it's time for you to have a special job to do. Would you put yourself in charge of Jacqueline—be her special protector? You know, when she goes to kindergarten no bully will ever dare to bother her because all she'll have to do is threaten to tell you, her big brother! We'll talk about it when I see you."[1]

When Jacqui came home, everyone smothered her with attention— except Ned. He busied himself composing this lullaby for her: "Go to sleep, little creep, / I'm tired and I'm beat. / Go to sleep, little creep, / before I drop you."

In 1967, Ned's attitude began to change. Dedi noticed that Ned's eyes were streaked with yellow. *Uuuueeee!* one kid squealed, "You got a yellow spider weaving a web around your eyeballs!" A blood test revealed that Ned had hepatitis and must be confined to bed.

Only Jacqui delighted in the diagnosis. Now she'd have her favorite "big brova" home with her all the time. Although a folding gate served as a barrier to entering Ned's room, Jacqui camped just outside the door to be with Ned. She insisted they have her third birthday party in the hallway so Ned could be included.

Meanwhile, Ned grew worse and was admitted to the hospital. For Jacqui, this was devastating. Even in a family bigger than the *Brady Bunch,* life was lonely and the house felt empty with Ned gone.

Ned also missed Jacqui. She was replaced by a jungle of cold, glowing equipment operated by strangers. Still, he remained optimistic.

Only once did Ned's cheerful spirit sour. After two months, he announced, "I'm tired of being sick." Then he added, "Don't worry, Mom. Things always turn out all right."

But things weren't all right. On Thanksgiving morning, 1967, Ned Taylor died. The puzzled doctors performed an autopsy in hopes of discovering the cause of his death.

A year and a half later, the Taylors received a letter from a stranger, Dr. Israel Herbert Scheinberg, an expert in rare hereditary diseases. He claimed to know the cause of Ned's death—Wilson's disease (progressive hepatolenticular degeneration). First recognized by the British neurologist Kinnear Wilson in 1912, there was no test to detect this disease until the 1950s, when Dr. Scheinberg, along with Dr. David Gitlin, developed one at Harvard Medical School.[2]

Dr. Scheinberg explained that this rare, inherited disease is caused by a buildup of toxic quantities of copper in the brain, liver, and other organs. He said that the odds of passing along the faulty gene to a child are less than one in forty thousand. Nevertheless, he urged that a blood analysis be done on all the Taylor children.

The blood test confirmed that Jacqui also had Wilson's disease. Fortunately, it wasn't too late. With medication and a strict diet, she could expect a normal life!

Following the test results, Edward and Dedi talked of Jacqui's close encounter with death. "It was Ned who saved her, you know," Edward said. "Without the tissue from his body, they never would have diagnosed her case in time."

"Yes, I know," Dedi replied. "Remember the letter I wrote Ned, asking him to take care of his baby sister?"

"I remember."

"Who could have known how well he would do just that?"

Months later, Jacqui and Mom visited Ned's grave. There Dedi shared with Jacqui the story of how the disease had been diagnosed only after Ned had died.

Shortly after that visit, Dedi wrote this in her journal: "Sadness and a sense of loss will forever be a part of my being. But that day with Jacqui—sunbeams dancing off her long, shining hair, sturdy legs bent as she concentrated on digging a proper hole for a chrysanthemum plant—I felt the sweet, sad joy of acceptance, of having come to terms with life."[3] Ned's death had indirectly given Jacqui the gift of life.

You, too, can come to terms with life—*eternal* life. For the sacrifice of Jesus has been complete. "Christ purchased you at an infinite cost," writes Ellen White. "He says to the Father. 'Here is a poor sinner. I have given My life for him. He is saved by My grace. Receive him as Your child.' Do you think the Father will refuse?"[4]

Of this you can be certain: the Father will not reject you after giving His only Son to redeem you. The Cross boldly declares the good news that there is no reason to feel uncertain as you stand before the Judge. You can face your eternal future with no doubt.

This assurance of salvation is illustrated in the movie *End of the Spear.* It tells the true story of five missionaries in the 1950s who died while trying to share the gospel with the violent Waodoni tribe in the Ecuadorian jungles. A fearless man named Nate Saint inspired his team of missionaries to reach out to the Waodoni, who were repeatedly involved in intertribal warfare.

In one scene, Nate's family gathers around him on the dirt airstrip in front of their house. As he is telling his family goodbye, his son, Steve, spots a rifle in his father's plane. Concerned, he asks his father, "If the Waodoni attack, will you use your guns? Will you defend yourselves?"

Unflinchingly, Nate answers Steve, "Son, we can't shoot the Waodoni. They're not ready for heaven. We are."[5]

Can you speak with the same certainty about being ready for heaven? The apostle Paul lived with this assurance of his eternal future. He wrote, "Now we look forward with confidence to our heavenly bodies" (2 Corinthians 5:6, TLB).

Do you have this confidence? You can! How? Accept Jesus Christ as your Savior and you will be saved (1 John 5:12, 13). "It is by grace you have been saved, through faith—and this not from yourselves, it is the gift of God—not by works, so that no one can boast" (Ephesians 2:8, 9).

His Spilled Blood

"This is my blood of the covenant,
which is poured out for many
for the forgiveness of sins."
—Matthew 26:28

Miles

By Nichole Nordeman and Kelly St. John

S OME YEARS AGO, NBC'S TELEVISION SHOW DATELINE FOLLOWED THE STORIES
of nine patients in ward 7E at Mount Sinai Hospital in New York City. These men
and women with failing hearts were waiting for new hearts to replace their failing
ones. Toward the end of the series, the producers captured the joy and elation of the patients
who received new hearts through successful transplants. Yet, the joy was bittersweet because
those new hearts came at the cost of others' lives. For one to live, another had to die.[1]

Such is our story. For you and me to live, Christ had to die.

This gospel truth is captured in the story of Miles Coulson. Born March 30, 2004, he
weighed in at a robust eleven pounds, six ounces, and measured twenty-two inches long. Two
weeks later, however, Miles stopped feeding. His skin was mottled; his arms and legs were
cold. What followed was every parent's nightmare: months of hospital stays for little Miles.
A virus caused myocarditis, an inflammation of the heart. Doctors never sugarcoated the
prognosis: Miles had a two-thirds chance of death—or, at best, compromised heart function.

Miles's story inspired Christian recording artist Nichole Nordeman to capture his
story in a song. Following the lyrics to her song is an article from the San Francisco
Chronicle that tells the rest of the story.

Miles

By Nichole Nordeman

There's a mother on her knees
somewhere in San Francisco
looking up and begging please
God, do not forget me now

Her baby's on machines
'cause his heart can not keep beating
and she knows what desperate means
'cause the clock is ticking down, down

and hope rushed in like waves
that someone might just save the day
and if heaven's just a prayer away
then why, she cries, would God not change things?

It may be miles and miles before the journey's clear
there may be rivers, may be oceans of tears
but the very hand that shields your eyes from understanding
is the hand that will be holding you for miles

There's another mother on her knees
somewhere in San Francisco
looking up and begging please
God, do not forget me now

It happened like a dream
he was laughing, he was running
then she heard the sirens scream
when her little boy fell down, down

She had never known
the agony of letting go
but a few miles down the road
his heart would find a baby boy just in time

One moment someone whispers thank you
just then another heart cries, how could you?
when Jesus, who sees us, He says I hear you
I'm near you

It may be miles and miles before the journey's clear
there may be rivers, may be oceans of tears
but the very hand that shields your eyes from understanding
is the Hand that will be holding you for miles.[2]

It was a touching tale that grabbed headlines. Little Miles Coulson, just five months old, was saved by a heart transplant over Labor Day weekend after his doctors had kept him alive with a heart pump imported from Germany.

The photographs of Miles—with his cheeky, open-mouthed smile—touched many people. But perhaps no one felt their tug more than Pamela Jimenez, thirty-nine, the San Francisco mother whose dead son helped Miles live.

Alexander Robert Sanchez was eleven months old, a chubby baby who was so big his uncle lovingly called him "the Tank."

Alex was playing in a walker at his aunt's house in San Francisco on September 3 when he fell onto a wooden floor, knocking his head and pulling a chair down on top of him. When the ambulance arrived, he had stopped breathing. He was rushed to San Francisco General Hospital, where his brain began to swell dangerously, Jimenez said.

It was clear he was going to die, she said, and she decided she would donate his organs.

She was motivated in part because Alex had his own medical problems. He was born with a condition called imperforate anus, meaning he lacked a normal anal opening. It happens in about one in five thousand births. Alex had had several surgeries to correct the problem—one at just two days old—and recovered in an intensive care unit.

She remembers meeting one mother there whose baby had a hole in her heart. Their only hope was a transplant. "I thought at the time, *that's so sad,*" she said.

By Sunday, two doctors had pronounced Alex brain-dead. Jimenez and her husband, Javier Sanchez, held Alex's body for the last time. Then doctors removed his heart, lungs, pancreas, liver, kidneys, and corneas, rushing them to hospitals across Northern California.

Jimenez learned that Miles received Alex's heart when news reports mentioned the heart came from an eleven-month-old child. She said she was comforted—not upset—at learning his name, and she encourages other parents in a similar tragedy to donate their children's organs.

"It has helped my grieving," Jimenez said. "Even though it is not my child, a part of my son is still physically alive. The gift of life is a wonderful thing, and to give the gift of life is even better."

Helen Christensen of the California Transplant Donor Network, which acts as a bridge between donor families and organ recipients, said donor families and recipients who want to communicate with each other often exchange anonymous letters.

Sometimes they eventually meet, but only if they want to learn each others' identities. Face-to-face meetings usually take place six months to a year or more after a transplant operation.

Miles's mother, Leigh Bills, said she was touched to learn Alex's identity and is grateful his parents not only made the difficult decision to donate his heart but are speaking publicly about the importance of organ donation.

Bills said she plans to write to Jimenez through the California Transplant Donor Network. She's still deciding exactly what she wants to say.

"It's a tremendous gift, and we can't come up with words to thank them,"

Bills said. "It's such a wonderful time for us because we can start to plan for the future. But the only reason we get to look at our future in a bright way is because they lost their child."[3]

For believers in Christ, the only reason our futures look bright is that our Father lost His Child.

"This is how much God loved the world: He gave his Son, his one and only Son. And this is why: so that no one need be destroyed; by believing in him, anyone can have a whole and lasting life. God didn't go to all the trouble of sending his Son merely to point an accusing finger, telling the world how bad it was. He came to help, to put the world right again. Anyone who trusts in him is acquitted; anyone who refuses to trust him has long since been under the death sentence without knowing it. And why? Because of that person's failure to believe in the one-of-a-kind Son of God when introduced to him" (John 3:16–18, *The Message*).

A Satisfied Thirst

By Max Lucado

T HIS WELL-WORN STORY WAS MADE POPULAR BY BEST-SELLING AUTHOR MAX
Lucado. In my opinion, it beautifully captures the essence of sacrificing love.

~

"Mommy, I'm so thirsty. I want a drink."

Susanna Petroysan heard her daughter's pleas, but there was nothing she could do. She and four-year-old Gayaney were trapped beneath tons of collapsed concrete and steel. Beside them in the darkness lay the body of Susanna's sister-in-law, Karine, one of the fifty-five thousand victims of the worst earthquake in the history of Soviet Armenia. . . .

Susanna had gone to Karine's house to try on a dress. It was December 7, 1988, at 11:30 A.M. The quake hit at 11:41. She had just removed the dress and was clad in stockings and a slip when the fifth-floor apartment began to shake. Susanna grabbed her daughter but had taken only a few steps before the floor opened up and they tumbled in. Susanna, Gayaney, and Karine fell into the basement with the nine-story apartment house crumbling around them.

"Mommy, I need a drink. Please give me something."

There was nothing for Susanna to give.

She was trapped flat on her back. A concrete panel eighteen inches above her head and a crumpled water pipe above her shoulders kept her from standing. Feeling around in the darkness, she found a twenty-four ounce jar of blackberry jam that had fallen into the basement. She gave the entire jar to her daughter to eat. It was gone by the second day.

"Mommy, I'm so thirsty."

Susanna knew she would die, but she wanted her daughter to live. She found a dress, perhaps the one she had come to try on, and made a bed for Gayaney. Though it was bitter cold, she took off her stockings and wrapped them around the child to keep her warm.

The two were trapped for eight days.

Because of the darkness, Susanna lost track of time. Because of the cold, she lost the feeling in her fingers and toes. Because of her inability to move, she lost hope. "I was just waiting for death." . . .

"Mommy, I'm thirsty."

At some point in that eternal night, Susanna had an idea. She remembered a television program about an explorer in the Arctic who was dying of thirst. His comrade slashed open his hand and gave his friend his blood.

"I had no water, no fruit juice, no liquids. It was then I remembered I had my own blood."

Her groping fingers, numb from the cold, found a piece of shattered glass. She sliced open her left index finger and gave it to her daughter to suck.

The drops of blood weren't enough. "Please, Mommy, some more. Cut another finger." Susanna has no idea how many times she cut herself. She only knows that if she hadn't, Gayaney would have died. Her blood was her daughter's only hope.[1]

✧

New Blood, New Life

B EFRIEND DEMI-LEE BRENNAN ON FACEBOOK AND YOU'LL THINK THAT you're scrolling through a typical teenager's life. She graduated from Kiama High School in 2008. She calls Albion Park, New South Wales, Australia, her home. For music, she loves everyone from Michael Jackson to Placebo. *The Hangover, How to Be a Serial Killer,* and *The Land Before Time* get the top three slots under "Movies." No surprises for television: *Seinfeld, Friends, Family Guy,* and so on. She's in a relationship, has 369 friends, and cites Bob Marley, "Truth is, everybody is going to hurt you; you just gotta find the ones worth suffering for."

Yep, Demi's your average kid. Well, except for the part on her Facebook page that mentions her as the "one-in-6-billion miracle" girl.[1] The odds of her being alive are about the same as shopping alone in Best Buy on Black Friday. "She should be dead," commented one skeptic.[2] "Wow, unheard of and almost unbelievable," quipped another.[3]

Demi-Lee was nine years old when a virus destroyed her liver. Doctors gave her less than forty-eight hours to live. Miraculously, a liver from a twelve-year-old boy arrived at the Children's Hospital at Westmead just in time.

But the miracles were only beginning. "When she was admitted to intensive care, she was very sick, and yellow," recalls her mom, Kerrie Mills. "We were told we were losing her."[4]

The outlook was bleak. In medical circles, liver transplants are dubbed the "last resort" and "the holy grail" of transplants. This is particularly true in a life-threatening case where it is impossible to find an ideal donor.

But Demi-Lee survived the ten-hour operation. Her ailing body was pumped full of immunosuppressant drugs, the poisonous cocktail for "transplant patients to ensure their bodies do not reject the donated organ."[5] Somehow, she beat the odds.

The biggest miracle, however, was still to come. "Nine months later, Demi-Lee developed life-threatening anemia" and had to be readmitted to the hospital. "Tests showed that stem cells from the new liver had migrated to her bone marrow (the site where blood cells are produced)." In desperation, the doctors resorted to an extreme measure—they halted Demi-Lee's antirejection therapy, thus allowing the donor cells to take over her own.[6]

"Oh, we were stunned, because we'd never come across this before," reported Dr. Michael Stormon, a pediatric hepatologist at Westmead. "There was no precedent for this having happened at any other time, so we were sort of flying by the seat of our pants."[7]

Indeed, the impossible happened. Demi-Lee's blood type had changed!

The head of hematology, "Julie Curtin, said she was stunned when she realized Demi-Lee was now O-positive, rather than O-negative. 'I was convinced we had made a mistake, so we tested it again and it came up the same. Then we tested her parents, and they were both O-negative, so it was confirmed that Demi absolutely had to have been O-negative.' "[8]

"Pediatric nephrologist, Dr. Stephen Alexander, says he wasn't easily convinced. 'We didn't believe this at first. We thought it was too strange to be true. . . . Normally the body's own immune system rejects any cells that are transplanted . . . but for some reason the cells that came from the donor's liver seemed to survive better than Demi-Lee's own cells.' "[9]

Dr. Stuart Dorney, the former head of Westmead's liver transplant unit, called it a "medical miracle" and said there is no explanation for what occurred. "We now need to go back over everything that happened to Demi and see why and if it can be replicated."[10]

For Demi-Lee, the miracle of her transformed immune system meant that she could stop taking the toxic antirejection drugs. No other liver transplant recipient in the world has been so lucky.

Today, Demi-Lee leads an ordinary life. She loves sports and dreams of competing on *Australian Idol*. And she bubbles with gratitude. "I'm probably the most grateful person because that has saved my life, that gave me a chance to fulfill my life. . . . I just want to live it the most I've got for [the doctors and the liver donor] and to show them that I'm so grateful."[11]

"I feel quite normal," she reports. "It's almost like it never happened. . . . I can't thank the donor's family enough, and the doctors, for giving me this second chance at life."[12]

The transplant not only extended her life, but it also changed it. The miracle transformed the very source of her life.

Her story is like our story. Because of sin, we, too, are staring at certain death. To redeem us, Jesus shed His blood at Calvary. Thanks to His blood, we can claim life—*eternal* life. It is the ultimate second chance!

But understand this: the spilled blood of Christ was not just a legal transaction that puts us in right standing with God. It is so much more. His blood enters into our lives and changes our very DNA. Jesus didn't just fix us. He changed us. In the end, this is the biggest miracle of all. We can experience new life in Christ.

"How much more is done by the blood of Christ. He offered himself through the eternal Spirit as a perfect sacrifice to God. His blood will make our consciences pure from useless acts so we may serve the living God" (Hebrews 9:14, NCV).

Sacrifice

By Carl Cosaert and Mark Witas

*S*INCE 2006, *I HAVE KEPT A PICTURE OF MINDY COSAERT UNDER THE GLASS ON my desk. Almost every day, I glance at the smiling face of this beautiful sixteen-year-old whose life was tragically cut short in a drowning accident on the Wenatchee River at Tumwater Canyon near Leavenworth, Washington.*

Her father, Carl Cosaert, who was attending an international Bible conference for Adventist theologians in Turkey at the time, shared his grief in the Adventist Review:

Not knowing what had happened and being 7,000 miles from home, I was overwhelmed by fear and helplessness. When I eventually reached my wife by phone, I learned that our daughter had been in an accident on a Sabbath afternoon trip to the river with the church youth group. Mindy and a friend had decided to float across what they had thought was a harmless part of the river, and were caught by an unexpectedly strong current that propelled them down a nearly mile-long stretch of intense rapids not visible from where they had been swimming. Her friend emerged with only a few scratches. My daughter was not so fortunate. She was found floating facedown in the river after being underwater for some 15 minutes. Although CPR revived a pulse, Mindy remained unconscious, struggling to breathe with first one, and then two, collapsed lungs. She was placed on life support at the hospital. . . .

After a lonely night in Amsterdam and a grueling flight back to Washington State, I finally made it to my little girl's side—nearly 48 hours after I first heard the news. I cried over her, hugged her, and gave her the pink scarf that I had bought specially for her in Turkey. I was hoping against hope that she would hear my voice and open her eyes, but there was no response. She was already brain dead. I learned later that she had actually been declared legally dead at 12:45 P.M. earlier that afternoon—five hours before I arrived.[1]

Years later, when I now see Mindy's picture, I am taken back to that time in my life when I grieved with Mindy's family and friends over her untimely death. The picture also triggers the memory of another young woman—Meghan Doggett, the "daughter" of my friends Mark and Wendy Witas and a student at the university where I served as pastor. Meghan also drowned that day. Listen now to another father as he remembers his daughter.

When Wendy, Cole, and I moved to Wenatchee, we didn't know what God had in store for us, but we knew that we were open to whomever He placed in our lives. It turns out, He had quite a plan.

My first encounter with Meghan was in the gymnasium at Cascade Christian Academy. I had just become one of the pastors at a church in Wenatchee, and I wanted to attend registration at the local Christian school. The only person I knew in the whole valley was Gene Roemer, the history teacher at the school. So I sat next to him, saying hi to all the students and parents who checked in at his table.

Shortly after I arrived, a 12-year-old boy came bouncing up to the table, looked at Gene, and said, "Hi, Dad."

I looked at Gene and said, "I didn't know you had a son!"

"I don't," he said. "This isn't a boy—it's a girl, and she's a senior in high school."

Meghan looked devastated that I thought she was a boy, but she shook it off and told me that it happened all the time.

Soon after I met her, I started to hear Meghan's story. When she was 9 years old, the police came into her home, arrested her mother and father, and separated the children into foster care. Evidently there had been some sort of organized ring of adults who had been abusing children, and Meghan was a witness for the prosecution.

The town of Wenatchee was split as to whether the people being accused of these heinous crimes were guilty or if there was a witch hunt to indict innocent people. The result was torturous to little Meghan. She was being picked on at school every day. Every day she would come home in tears, begging her foster mom not to make her go back to school the next day.

Finally, in an act of desperation, Meghan's foster family approached Cascade Christian Academy and enrolled her there.

It was during Meghan's senior year that Meghan sat me down for a serious talk. She said, "This school and this church are family to me, and I want this to be a part of my family from now on. Would you baptize me? I want to be a part of this church and school family for the rest of my life."

It was my privilege to study Scripture with Meghan and watch her develop an absolutely precious relationship with her Creator. And it was also my privilege to walk out into the ocean at Rosario Beach near Anacortes, Washington, on a school-sponsored spiritual retreat and baptize her in front of her school family.

It wasn't long after that that Meghan started spending more and more time with Wendy, Cole, and me. I don't recall ever inviting her over—she'd just show up and stay for a few days at a time.

While in our home, Meghan began to share her life story with me, and it was during that time that she began to worm her way into the heart and life of our family.

Meghan moved into our home. Again, I don't remember inviting her—she just showed up with her stuff one day. Actually, she went behind my back and had my wife convinced that she needed to come live with us. My wife is such a softy.

It wasn't long after she moved in that she sat Wendy and me down and told us that she wanted to start calling us "Mom and Dad."

I felt pretty uncomfortable with that, and I told her so. Meghan said, "I guess it doesn't matter to me if you feel uncomfortable about that, because that's what I'm calling you now."

While she lived with us, she became the daughter we never had. She shared her deepest joys, fears, hopes, dreams, and frustrations with us. She cheated at cards, rearranged her room 348 times, and gave the deepest shoulder and back rubs a person could experience without yelling in pain. She learned to drive, and we helped her purchase a car. She learned to work and got several jobs.

Meghan also became involved in her church in a way that would make most church-going adults hang their head in shame. She learned to love, and she shared that love with Wendy, Cole, and me. She made a pledge not to go down the road of substance abuse, tobacco, or alcohol. She figured life was too short and too precious to hand it over to something that could destroy her so fast.

Her diet consisted of candy, Life cereal, and uncooked Top Ramen. She loved oranges, but hated the taste of strawberries, peaches, and nectarines.

Every Sunday she'd mow the lawn, and every Sunday night she'd say, "Dad, you owe me 20 bucks." I'd tell her she missed a spot, and she would roll her eyes and hold out her hand.

Wendy, Cole, and I had plans with Meghan. We wanted to take her to Africa with us to go on safari and see the animals on the Masai Mara. We wanted to see her achieve in school and become the social worker she longed to become. We wanted to see her marry and have children of her own. We had plans.

Nothing crushed her like the times I expressed disappointment in a decision she had made. Nothing made her glow like the times I told her I loved her and was proud of her.

Well, I couldn't love her or be more proud of the actions she took on her last Sabbath afternoon.

Meghan and a large group of youth were sitting alongside a river in the sun. Some people were swimming, while some were sitting and playing guitars. It was a perfect afternoon for lounging and enjoying one another's company. Two of the girls in the group had dozed off on an air mattress and had drifted to a dangerous end of the swimming hole toward some rapids that led to a torrential part of the river. Some men on the adjacent bank yelled a warning. That's when Meghan jumped to her feet and started running down the beach with the obvious intent to dive in and save the two young ladies.

Jesus said, "Greater love hath no man than this, that a man lay down his life for his friends" [John 15:13, KJV].

When we went up to the river this week, I found a rock that was stained with Meghan's blood. As I stood and looked at it, something dawned on me. Meghan and Jesus have something in common. Both of them spilled their blood in an attempt to save someone they loved and cared about.

The last time I saw Meghan was when she dropped me at the airport on Thursday night before the weekend she gave her life. We stood at the side of the car, and she hugged me tight and said, "I love you, Dad."

I said, "I love you, too."

The next time I see Meghan will be at the resurrection. She'll run to me and say, "I love you, Dad."

I'll hug her and say, "I love you, too."

We're so proud of her, and we miss her dearly. It just makes me all the more eager for Jesus to return, because resurrection morning is going to be a great reunion for me and my family.[2]

❧

Terror at the Taj

A s September 11, 2001, is to Americans, so November 26, 2008, is to Indians. Commonly referred to as 26/11, the date marks the beginning of a sixty-hour tour of carnage carried out by Pakistani terrorists. A highly trained, well-equipped team masterminded eleven coordinated attacks across Mumbai, India's largest city, killing 164 people and wounding at least 308.[1]

The *Los Angeles Times* reported on the first day of the siege: "The attackers swept through two luxury hotels favored by foreigners, the Taj Mahal Palace and the Oberoi, firing automatic weapons, throwing grenades and sending panicked guests scrambling for safety. Some guests were trapped inside the hotels for hours, even as a series of explosions set fire to the Taj hotel, a landmark along Mumbai's waterfront."[2]

One of the one thousand guests and five hundred employees trapped inside the Taj Mahal Palace and Tower was Maria Mooers, a Texas oil heiress. She watched helplessly through her window as a man was trapped in a burning room. Soon smoke seeped under her door.

All that day and the next day, Maria was on her phone—perched in a prison at ground zero. When commandos finally arrived to rescue her, Maria says, "They threw me over their shoulder like a trussed turkey. . . . They said, 'Give us some water. We have not had a drop to drink. Move quickly. Close your eyes. There are terrorists in the hall.' " They escaped to the stairwell amid whizzing bullets. Maria remembers bodies and blood all over the floor.[3]

Other guests were trapped in one of the hotel's five-star restaurants. In his book *Has Christianity Failed You?* Ravi Zacharias tells of one diner:

> After the carnage . . . one of the guests who had been at the hotel for dinner that night was interviewed by the media. An Indian-born English actor, he described how he and his friends were eating dinner when they heard gunshots. Someone grabbed him and pulled him under the table. The assassins came striding through the restaurant, shooting at will, until everyone (so they thought) had been killed. This man, however, found

himself miraculously alive. When the interviewer asked him how it was that everyone at his table and in the room was dead and yet he was alive, his answer was sobering: "I suppose it's because I was covered in someone else's blood, and they took me for dead."[4]

Zacharias goes on to say, "This is a perfect metaphor of God's gift through Jesus to each one of us. Because he paid the penalty for our sin—because we are covered in the blood of his sacrifice—we may have eternal life."[5]

A similar snapshot is recorded in Exodus 12. God instructed the Hebrew slaves to smear the blood of slaughtered lambs around the doorposts of their homes. Seeing the blood, the angel of death would spare their lives. God explained, "The blood will be a sign for you on the houses where you are, and when I see the blood, I will pass over you" (Exodus 12:13).

"When I see the blood, I will pass over you." Now that will provide a good sermon topic at any Communion service, don't you agree?

That blood prefigured the blood of Christ. Peter explained, "You know that it was not with perishable things such as silver or gold that you were redeemed from the empty way of life handed down to you from your ancestors, but with the precious blood of Christ, a lamb without blemish or defect" (1 Peter 1:18, 19).

In her last recorded letter, Ellen White wrote,

God is waiting to bestow the blessing of forgiveness, of pardon for iniquity, of the gifts of righteousness, upon all who will believe in His love and accept the salvation He offers. Christ is ready to say to the repenting sinner, "Behold, I have caused thine iniquity to pass from thee, and I will clothe thee with change of raiment." The blood of Jesus Christ is the eloquent plea that speaks in behalf of sinners. This blood "cleanseth us from all sin."[6]

❧

His Sacrificial Love

"Greater love has no one than this:
to lay down one's life for one's friends."
—John 15:13

Girl Against a Blizzard

By Helen Rezatto

T HIS WAS THE STORY THAT MY FATHER'S FORMER HEAD ELDER, MR. CARPEN-
*ter, could remember twenty-five years after hearing it for the first—and only—
time. Although I have heard Dad share this story several times in various churches,
it remains a vivid and moving memory to think of Hazel Miner's sacrifice and my father's
emotion in sharing it.*

The morning of March 15 was pleasant and sunny as William Miner, a farmer
near Center, N.D., completed his chores. A thaw had set in, and the snow in the
fields was patchy.

"Snow should be gone by night," he reported optimistically to his wife
when he came in at noon. After the couple had eaten a leisurely meal, Miner
glanced out the kitchen window. "Good Lord!" he exclaimed.

In the northwest a black, billowy cloud loomed over the horizon. It moved
stealthily, inexorably, its dark bluish edges spreading across the sky toward the
unsuspecting sun.

Blanche Miner spoke with the sure instinct of a homesteader, "A spring
norther!"

They watched the advance of the formless, faceless monster. Abruptly, Miner
said, "You get the stock in. I'm going to school to get the kids. I don't like the
looks of it."

Miner piled on his storm clothes, saddled Kit, his best horse, and started
down the slushy road to the school two and a half miles away. By now the
apparition had writhed and swelled its way to overpower the sun. All nature
was poised, breathless, apprehensive. Then an avalanche of blinding snow and
wind slammed into the horse and rider. Miner fought through it to the school
barn, tied Kit among the other stomping, nervous horses, and hurried into the
schoolhouse.

The teacher and pupils had observed the approach of the blizzard, but were
still pretending to concentrate on lessons. Although many children had their

own horses and sleighs in the school barn, the established blizzard rule was that no child should leave unless called for by a parent.

"Hi, Dad!" fifteen-year-old Hazel Miner exclaimed. She turned to her brother, Emmet, eleven, and her sister, Myrdith, eight. "I guess *somebody* doesn't trust us to drive old Maude home!"

Her father smiled briefly. "Hurry! Get your wraps—here are extra scarves."

Hazel bent down to fasten her sister's overshoes and said to Emmet, "Don't forget your history book." *Hazel is wonderfully dependable,* Miner thought. *She always far surpassed expectations.*

Dad carried Myrdith outside to their homemade sleigh with its rounded canvas cover, settled the two children in the straw lining the bottom, covered them with two blankets and an old fur robe. Then Hazel perched on the driver's seat while her father hitched Maude to the sleigh. Above the belligerent wind he shouted to Hazel, "Stay right here! I'll get Kit and lead the way."

Maude was facing the north gate toward home. She had always been placid and easily managed, but now a thunderclap startled her, and she bolted, swerving through the south gate. Hazel, knocked off balance and hardly able to see through the swirling snow, did not realize at first that Maude was headed in the wrong direction. She shouted to the wide-eyed younger children, "Don't worry, we'll beat Dad and Kit home! Maude knows the way."

Hazel could do nothing to control the horse, for the reins trailed out of reach beneath the tugs. Finally, Maude slowed to a walk and stopped, her sides heaving.

Emmet called, "Are we home? Did we beat Dad?"

Hazel stepped down into the snow. Through the dizzying gloom she could not tell whether they were on a road or in a field. The whole world had become a white-foaming, lashing sea, threatening to swallow them all. Panting for breath, she crawled back into the driver's seat with the reins. "No, we're not home yet, but I think we're close. Now that Maude's calmed down, she'll know the way."

Maude, repentant about her escapade, plowed along through the growing gloom. Once she plunged into a low place filled with water from the spring thaws and choked with ice and new snow. A tug came unhitched, and Hazel stepped down into the chilling slush, reached her bare hands into the water, fumbled for the tug, fastened it. By the time she led Maude out of the water, she was soaked to the waist and her clothes were turning into heavy armor.

Then, close by, she saw the top of a fence post sticking above the snow. She dug into the snow until she located the barbed wire. The fence would lead them to a farm and safety.

Emmet got out to see what she was doing. Together, they broke off the crystal mask that had formed over Maude's face. They grasped Maude's bridle to keep her on the fence line, but a huge drift blocked the way and they had to turn off the course. Frantically trying to get back, Emmet and Hazel pawed for the wire or another post to guide them. They could find neither. (The gate, buried in the big drift, opened to a farm only 200 feet away.)

Almost suffocated from the onslaught of wind and snow, the two climbed back into the sleigh. Stubbornly, Maude kept on until the sleigh lurched over a concealed obstacle. It tipped over on its side, and the children were thrown against the canvas top.

Again Hazel and Emmet got out. Blindly, they pushed, they heaved, they pulled. The sleigh, jammed into the snow, was too heavy for them to right.

In the howling darkness, Hazel realized that she must think—it was up to her, the oldest. She fumbled inside the canvas. "See," she said, "we're in a little cave. We'll fix it nice and cozy."

Since the sleigh was on its side, the narrow wooden floor formed a low wall to the east and the canvas top, uncurtained at the ends, made a tunnel-like tent. In the dark, Hazel found the blankets and robe. Despite her now-crippled hands, she placed the two blankets on the canvas "floor." Following her instructions, Emmet and Myrdith lay down, curled together tightly. The wind snarled through the north opening, and Hazel tried to improvise a curtain with the fur robe. It blew down again and again. Finally she tucked the robe around her brother and sister.

The hellish wind tore and ripped at the canvas top. Hazel snatched at the flapping scraps and piled over the robe all that she could salvage. There was only one way to keep them in place—to fling herself on top of them. Now there was nothing between the three children and the blizzard except some dangling strips blowing from the bare wooden framework.

The snow fell incessantly. Three human specks lay motionless, their minds and bodies stupefied, benumbed by the terrifying, pulsating forces. Hazel roused herself. "Emmet! Myrdith!" she shouted. "You mustn't close your eyes. Punch each other. I'll count to a hundred. Make your legs go up and down as though you're running. Begin—one, two, three—" She could feel the small limbs moving underneath her. She tried to move her own; her brain instructed her legs, but she wasn't sure what they did.

"I'm tired. Can't we stop?" begged Myrdith's muffled voice.

"No!" came the stern answer. "We're only at seventy-one."

Next Hazel ordered, "Open and close your fingers one hundred times inside your mittens."

Emmet stuck his head out from under the robe. "Come on, Hazel, get under here. We'll make room."

"No, I can't." Little warmth her ice-mantled clothes would provide the others. "Everything blows away. I've got to hold it down. Besides, I'm not very cold. Let's sing 'America, the Beautiful' like in opening exercises this morning."

From underneath the robe came the thin, childish voices and the words they had sung only that morning—but a hundred years away. *For purple mountain majesties above the fruited plain.* They sang all four verses.

"Let's pray to God to help us," suggested Myrdith. " 'Now I lay me down to sleep—' " she began.

Hazel interrupted, "No, not that one. Let's say 'Our Father' instead." Solemnly they chanted the prayer.

On into the timeless night, Hazel directed them—in exercises, stories, songs, prayers. Several times she sat up in the never-ending snow and forced her nearly paralyzed fingers to break the crusts that formed around Myrdith's and Emmet's legs; then she brushed and scraped away the creeping menace.

She said to the two children over and over, "Remember, you mustn't go to sleep—even if I do. Promise me you won't, no matter how sleepy you get. *Keep each other awake!* Promise?"

They promised.

More than once Myrdith voiced the question: "Why doesn't Daddy find us?"

When William Miner discovered his children had disappeared from the schoolyard, he urged Kit mercilessly through the fast forming drifts, sure that Maude had gone home. His wife met him at the door. They gazed, stricken, into each other's eyes.

Immediately, he gave the alarm over the rural party lines. Nearly forty men, risking their lives, were soon moving slowly, persistently, over the fields and roads between Miner's farm and the school. They paused at farms to change teams, to treat frostbite, to gulp coffee, to devise new plans. All the other children were safe in their homes. The men found nothing.

The wind became a sixty-mile-an-hour gale, the temperature dropped to zero, the gray became utter blackness. And the maddening snow kept falling. The searchers had to give up until daylight.

Next morning one group of searchers reported tracks made by a small sleigh and a horse that went out the south schoolhouse gate—then were obliterated by falling snow. Quickly, the search was reorganized. Men with teams and sleighs, men on horseback, men on foot fanned out for half a mile. Back and forth they forced their way across the shrouded land.

At two o'clock on Tuesday afternoon, twenty-five hours from the time the Miner children had disappeared, searchers spotted something in a pasture two miles south of the school. It was an overturned sleigh. Next to it, like a sentry, a ghostlike horse stood motionless, but still alive. They saw a bulky snow-covered mound under the arch of the naked, skeletonlike staves.

The rigid body of a girl lay face down with her unbuttoned coat flung wide. Her arms were stretched over her brother and sister, sheltering and embracing them in death as she had in life.

Tenderly, the men lifted her, then slowly removed the matted robe and torn canvas pieces that she had been holding down with her body. Underneath were Myrdith and Emmet, dazed and partially frozen, but alive. They had promised never to fall into the dread sleep from which Hazel knew they could never waken.

Today, on the courthouse grounds in the town of Center, these words are engraved on a granite monument rising, like a challenge, above the plains:

In
Memory
of
HAZEL MINER
April 11, 1904
March 16, 1920
To the dead a tribute
To the living a memory
To posterity an inspiration
THE STORY OF HER LIFE AND OF HER
TRAGIC DEATH IS RECORDED IN THE
ARCHIVES OF OLIVER COUNTY.
STRANGER, READ IT.[1]

A Life and Death of Service

O N A RECENT VISIT TO TOOWOOMBA, QUEENSLAND, AUSTRALIA, I RE-
searched and shared the story of its local hero, Jordan Rice, who—only days
before my arrival—gave his life to save his brother (see the chapter "The River
and Jordan"). While talking about Jordan at a local church, I mentioned that I was col-
lecting stories of human sacrifice for this project.

Following our meeting, Lynne Hughes introduced herself and said that her grandpa,
Trevor Collett, also gave his life for a friend. Handing me a stack of notes, she said, "We
would be thrilled if you were able to use the story of my grandfather for your book." Later
she e-mailed me: "Mum was so excited after talking to you, that maybe her dad's story
could be told. She went to sleep in her dad's arms when she was four—just before the
women and children were shipped down to Australia—and never saw him again."

Thank you, Lynne and Anthea, for sharing Trevor's story. It is a beautiful snapshot of
our Friend who laid down His life for us.

Trevor David Collett was only twenty-nine when he died. But his short life
packs a long legacy of sacrifice and service.

Born to wealthy landowners, Thomas and Lucretia Collett, Trevor was in line
to inherit the prosperous family farm strategically situated in Wee Waa, the rich
agricultural heartland that is dubbed the Cotton Capital of Australia.

An avid student of Scripture, Trevor acted upon his convictions to observe
the seventh-day Sabbath and joined the local Seventh-day Adventist church. This
decision infuriated his father, who promptly wrote Trevor out of the will.

Undaunted, Trevor enrolled at Australasian Missionary College to pursue
his dream of becoming a missionary to remote areas of New Guinea. Sharing
Trevor's vision of serving in far-off mission fields was his best friend, Bill Baines.
In 1934, Bill and Trevor dropped out of school to pursue this passion. Although
at first they wanted nothing to do with women or anything that might detract
from their calling to the mission field, Trevor could not resist a lovely young
woman named Olga Wiles, a person of uncompromising character who shared

his passion for service. When Bill met Trevor's younger sister Elwyn, he promptly forgot about his vow to never marry!

The two couples shared a dream of operating a plantation where workers were treated humanely and with the dignity befitting valued children of God—a rare scenario among plantation owners in New Guinea at that time. Part of the rhythm of plantation life there in Boliu, Mussau, included a day for Sabbath rest. While the workers were encouraged to enjoy a day reserved for God and family, every Saturday the Collett and Baines families hiked to the surrounding villages to share the gospel of Jesus.

In 1935, Trevor and Olga celebrated the birth of their first child. Tragically, their baby girl died a few days later at the hands of a drunken doctor who had crushed her skull with forceps. In 1937, Olga gave birth to another baby girl, aptly named Anthea, or "Lady of Flowers." She was indeed the flower of joy in the Collett home.

The next several years provided cherished family memories for the Colletts. They moved to Emira (now called Emirau Island), another small isle in the Mussau group of islands. They loved the lush environment of unpolluted warm water, golden beaches, living reefs, and tropical vegetation. Business was profitable on both the sawmill and the plantation sides of the operation. More important, the church was growing. The Colletts blended seamlessly into the Emiran culture.

During this time, Trevor and Olga continued to enjoy a close friendship with the Boliu mission director Arthur Atkins. This bond began on Mussau at Boliu and carried on long after the Colletts relocated to Emira. The friends enjoyed reconnecting whenever Arthur arrived with supplies. Trevor and Arthur loved to share updates about God's work advancing through the islands. On rare occasions, they would team up to go into the villages and share about Jesus. It helped that both men were fluent in the Mussau language.

Trevor and Olga took an active interest in the local people and had daily worship for their employees. For a season, life was as spiritually rich and as meaningful as the Colletts had always dreamed it would be.

But brewing on the global horizon was a political storm that would scar the tranquility in New Guinea forever. World War II erupted in all of its evil fury.

The wake-up call to world events came on Friday, December 20, 1940. German raider vessels circled the island three times, like hovering sharks. Soon, a messenger delivered the news that the three large German ships had anchored off the coast of Emira.

Three German captains, escorted by heavily armed soldiers, approached Trevor and inquired about the conditions of the place. "We have four hundred ninety-six prisoners who are survivors from sunken ships," the Germans explained to Trevor. "Is there enough food and water on the island to feed them all?"

One of the captains had been to Emira before—at a time when the islanders were notoriously savage cannibals. Trevor respected this captain and could appreciate his reticence to leave the prisoners of war (POWs) in an unsafe environment. Trevor assured him, however, that the islanders had changed. Emira was a safe place. He could unload his human cargo and move on to carry out

Hitler's orders to bomb Nauru and Ocean Islands. Loathing Hitler, the captain was delighted to drop off the hostages under the safekeeping of Trevor Collett rather than deliver them to torture chambers back home.

So it was that the 260 people living on Emira sprang into action to care for their unexpected visitors. The Colletts' plantation truck rumbled all night and most of the next day to transport the prisoners to the two European homes and to the village. According to Patovaki, a local teacher on the island, "The German soldiers killed all the chickens . . . and frightened the children. When the German ships had left, I told the people to gather food for the survivors. Pawpaws, coconuts, bananas, sweet potatoes, chickens, and fish were gathered in three hundred baskets."

Later, a grateful government expressed appreciation to the Colletts for their Christian hospitality. Peter Fraser, the prime minister of New Zealand, wrote the following:

Dear Mr. and Mrs. Collett,

I am writing to you in grateful acknowledgement from the Government and people of New Zealand for all that you did in looking after the survivors from the ships sunk by the German raiders.

I have not the slightest doubt that the unannounced influx of so many visitors to Emira Island and to your home would have been most inconvenient. The various groups of survivors who have been returned to New Zealand have, however, all said the same thing, that is they have spoken in the most appreciative terms of the wonderful kindness and hospitality of yourselves . . . and the way in which you spared no effort to make them comfortable and happy in their new surroundings. I am quite sure they will always retain the most pleasant recollections of their stay on the island; and I can assure you that the Government and the people of New Zealand will also retain the kindliest memories for what you did for them all. I would extend to you both the very best wishes for every happiness and prosperity in the future.

Yours faithfully,

P. Fraser

Prime Minister

This kind of selfless hospitality came naturally and often to Trevor Collett. A spirit of generous service marked him throughout his life—and especially in his death.

The war raged on, the world plunging deeper and deeper into darkness. As the threat of Japanese invasion grew, all expatriate women and children—including Olga and Anthea Collett—were forced to evacuate the island. Trevor remained in New Guinea, reluctant to abandon his people or his mission. By the end of 1941, however, the government ordered all expatriates on the island to return to Australia.

Having no other options, Arthur Atkins, Trevor Collett, and the remaining missionaries and expatriates boarded their ship, the *Malalangi,* to sail toward safety. Although sailing under the cover of night in a ship camouflaged in coconut fronds and banana palms, an astute Japanese fighter pilot reported seeing a "traveling island." When the pilot swooped low for a closer look, Trevor and his crew knew they had no option but to abandon ship, swim to shore, and retreat on foot toward the township of Rabaul in the province of East New Britain.

After the strenuous swim and an exhausting hike, Arthur fell violently ill. Plagued with severe asthma and unable to press on, he urged his friends, "Go, go, I beg you to go on without me." All of his friends obeyed his urging—all except Trevor.

"No," Trevor insisted. "Even if we have to surrender to the Japanese, we must get you medical care. I will not leave you to die alone."

"But, you must—" Arthur weakly protested.

Trevor was resolute. "I am staying with you. If we die, we die."

While their colleagues eventually returned safely to Australia, Trevor escorted Arthur to the town of Putput. Out of options and desperate, the men surrendered to the Japanese in return for medical care.

Hearing that Atkins was a missionary, the Japanese treated him kindly and did all they could to assure his comfort. For three weeks, Catholic nurses cared for Atkins with gentle compassion. But he was too sick. He died on March 13, 1942.

Years later, an attending physician would relate heroic tales of Atkins's selfless service to soldiers. The doctor wrote the following to Arthur's wife:

Dear Mrs. Atkins,

Your husband gave his life in succoring the sick soldiers at his station. I was told of his work by many who were brought in by the Japs at the same time. Mr. Atkins . . . was up night and day administering to the wants of those soldiers suffering from dysentery. . . . No truer words could be said than "He died for his fellow men."

Please accept my deepest sympathy.

Yours sincerely,

N. B. Watch

Indeed, no truer words could also be said for Arthur's friend Trevor Collett. He, too, gave his life for his fellowman.

When Atkins was transported to the hospital at Kokopo, as expected, Collett was arrested. For the next three months, he would be forced to do hard labor as a POW on the wharves.

On June 22, 1942, the Japanese ship *Montevideo Maru* left Rabaul's harbor with more than eight hundred POWs aboard. There were no markings on the ship to indicate that it carried POWs. On July 1, 1942, the American submarine *Sturgeon* torpedoed the boat just off Hainan Island near southern China. Historians continue to debate whether or not there were any survivors.

Years would elapse before Olga Collett would receive any official communication regarding her husband's disappearance. On a communiqué dated October 11, 1945, she read the following:

Dear Mrs. Collett,

Please find herewith for your information a copy of a statement by the Minister for External Territories regarding former New Guinea residents who have been reported missing.

It is desired to express the utmost sympathy in your present anxiety but you can rest assured that you will be advised at once when anything definite is established regarding your next of kin.

Yours sincerely,

A. J. Gaskin

Officer in Charge

Still preserved in Boliu is a hymnbook that Bill Baines, Trevor's best friend from college, created and delivered as a memorial to Trevor Collett. In the Mussau language, Bill wrote, "Dedicated to a special Christian friend. We don't really know what his end was but he showed that 'Greater love has no man than this, that a man lay down his life for his friend.' We will hold his memory close."

Of her grandpa, Lynne Hughes writes,

Grandpa left me with a powerful spiritual legacy: one that cost him dearly in earthly inheritance. His focus was to help and bless other people by his life—he did so as a fair plantation owner and by staying with his sick friend. He knew his God and served Him. He loved his friend enough to die for him. What a legacy! What a life!

Lynne once asked her grandma, Olga Collett, if she resented her husband dying at such a young age and so needlessly for a friend. "No," she replied softly, "he would never have been able to look himself in the mirror and would have classed himself the world's worst friend—if he hadn't made the choice to stay with Arthur. He would not have been the man I married if he hadn't chosen the route of unselfish love. I couldn't ask any different of him."

Rescue From an Icy Hell

J ANUARY 13, 2012, MARKED THE THIRTIETH ANNIVERSARY OF AIR FLORIDA *Flight 90 that crashed into the Fourteenth Street Bridge in Washington, D.C., shortly after takeoff. Over the decades (and as recently as last weekend when I listened to a sermon by Pastor Dwight Nelson from the Pioneer Memorial Seventh-day Adventist Church in Berrien Springs, Michigan), I have heard many preachers reference the wreck in telling the story of Arland D. Williams Jr. I share the story in the hope that it will be preserved for ages to come, as it provides a vivid reminder of the selfless sacrifice our Savior made in rescuing us from sure death.*

He died long before the advent of Facebook, but a page on the social networking site marks a memorial to him. There's no picture, just the basic facts:

> Arland Dean Williams Jr. (September 23, 1935–January 13, 1982) was a passenger aboard Air Florida Flight 90, which crashed on take-off in Washington, D.C., on January 13, 1982, killing 78 people. He was among the six people to initially survive the crash. His actions after the crash, handling the initial rescue efforts as a first responder, became a well-known example of extraordinary heroism, although it cost him his life. He did not know any of the other victims personally. In fact, his identity was not even known until some time after the bodies were recovered.[1]

Of course, there is so much more to the story of this forty-six-year-old senior examiner at the Federal Reserve Bank in Atlanta.

The plane's cockpit voice recorder captured the panic shared by the pilots only minutes after takeoff:

16:00:59 CAM-1   Stalling, we're falling!
16:01:00 CAM-2   This is it. We're going down, Larry. . . .

16:01:01 CAM-1   I know it!
16:01:01   [Sound of impact][2]

Next came the dramatic image of four survivors clinging to the Boeing 737's clipped tail section amid the ice floes. Then a fifth survivor bobbed to the surface. Together, they were lost in an arctic desert of jagged ice.

One eyewitness recalls the following:

There were a few pieces of the plane on shore that were smoldering and you could hear the screams of the survivors. More people arrived near the shore from the bridge but nobody could do anything. The ice was broken up and there was no way to walk out there. It was so eerie, an entire plane vanished except for a tail section, the survivors and a few pieces of plane debris. The smell of jet fuel was everywhere and you could smell it on your clothes. The snow on the banks was easily two feet high and your legs and feet would fall deep into it every time you moved from the water.[3]

Twenty minutes after the crash, a United States Park Police helicopter hovered over the harrowing scene. Emergency workers lowered a lifeline to Bert Hamilton, the first victim to be rescued from the numbing cold of the 31°F water.

The chopper returned. This time it was Arland's turn. But instead of clutching it for his own dear life, he passed the life ring to Kelly Duncan, a twenty-two-year-old flight attendant from Miami, Florida. She survived.

The helicopter returned and once again offered Arland an escape from the freezing hell. Again, he passed the line—this time to Joe Stiley. Although Stiley was severely injured, he managed to grasp, at least momentarily, another passenger, Priscilla Tirado. A second line was dropped; Patricia Felch quickly claimed it. But the weight of the three victims was too much and both Felch and Tirado dropped back into the polar Potomac. Thanks to the heroic efforts of two men willing to jump into the freezing fray, both Felch and Tirado were rescued.

Five lives had now been saved. When the helicopter returned for Williams, however, it was too late. Rescue officer Gene Windsor wept as he described the sacrifice that Williams had made: " 'He could have gone on the first trip, but he put everyone else ahead of himself. Everyone.' "[4]

The sentiments of a clergyman are quoted on the Facebook page for Arland Williams:

His heroism was not rash. Aware that his own strength was fading, he deliberately handed hope to someone else, and he did so repeatedly. On that cold and tragic day, Arland D. Williams Jr. exemplified one of the best attributes of human nature, specifically that some people are capable of doing "anything" for total strangers.[5]

One of those strangers, Kelly Duncan, would always be grateful for the sacrifice that Williams made for her. After returning as a flight attendant for a couple of years after the crash, Duncan switched careers and served with children's ministries in a local church. Then she received a degree in early childhood education and worked as a teacher. "I feel like every day has been a blessing," Duncan said in a 2005 CNN interview. "I have a wonderful life. . . . It sounds crazy to say it, but that accident changed my life for good. . . . God used a bad thing to turn my life around."[6]

On a Web site reporting the thirtieth anniversary of the crash, some writers shared their personal memories of the event. Wes Junker remembers, "My biggest recollection of the coverage was watching or hearing about one of the passengers who kept deferring his chance to get out of the cold waters to save a couple of other passengers. He ended up succumbing to the cold and drowned. He was a true hero."[7]

How can we forget this true hero?

Isn't that the best part of anniversaries? We get to pause and remember.

Similarly, whenever we gather at the Lord's table, we celebrate the anniversary of Jesus handing us His lifeline. The bread and juice are symbols to remind us that "Christ has rescued us from the curse pronounced by the law. When he was hung on the cross, he took upon himself the curse for our wrongdoing" (Galatians 3:13, NLT).

You and I are cursed to die. There is no escape. You may be impeccably orthodox and doctrinally pure, right down to your decaffeinated, nonalcoholic, smoke-free, vegan little soul—but you're still gonna die. Your only hope is to be rescued from the curse of the law.

The good news is that Jesus offers you a way out. Pastor Paul White explains,

> When Jesus died on the cross, He . . . took upon Himself the curse that accompanied the law. That curse could not come upon Jesus for His own law-breaking, for He had none, so it came upon Him because at Calvary, Jesus took our place. What was meant to come upon the whole of humanity was put upon Christ with full force at the cross. The curse was death, and its application on Jesus freed the rest of us from torment.[8]

The Cross is a towering memorial to the new life that we receive in Christ. It is a symbol of God's grand and glorious rescue of lost humanity.

On a personal note, the Cross is the passion of my heart—and the focus of my life. Like the apostle Paul, I determine "not to know anything among you except Jesus Christ and Him crucified" (1 Corinthians 2:2, NKJV).

On a recent business trip to Washington, D.C., I escaped an endless docket of meetings to reflect on the sacrifice of Jesus. Naturally, I went to the Fourteenth Street Bridge. It was repaired many years ago. Now, motorists cross over it without remembering what happened there more than thirty years ago.

But it's still my favorite place in town to reflect. There, I remembered, prayed, and thanked God for His redeeming narrative in my life.

Of course, it is no longer called the Fourteenth Street Bridge. Since 1983, it is officially known as the Arland D. Williams Jr. Memorial Bridge.

❧

Inmate 16670

R ECENTLY, A CHURCH MEMBER APPROACHED ME AND SAID, *"PASTOR, HAVE you ever heard the story about Father Kolbe?"* I told him that, yes, I was famil-iar with the story, very familiar in fact. It was one of the first stories my father would use when arriving in a new district.

"Why don't you tell that story some Sabbath?" he asked.

"I could," I said. *"I haven't shared it because I thought that everyone probably has already heard it."*

"I'm not so sure, Pastor. I read it for the first time just last week."

Although old and familiar, Father Kolbe's story remains a classic. So I have included it in this collection as a poignant reminder of another account of sacrifice.

Auschwitz. The very name evokes visceral angst. Rudolf Höss, the first com-manding officer at the camp, testified at the Nuremberg Trials that as many as three million people had perished there—a number later revised to 1.3 million.[1] Whatever the actual number of deaths, the German death camp has become synonymous with torture, death, and darkness. From this dungeon of despair, however, shines what Pope Paul VI would later describe as "the brightest and most glittering figure,"[2] referring to Maximilian Maria Kolbe.

Born Raymund Kolbe on January 8, 1894, this brilliant young man joined an order of friars and adopted the name Maximilian. As a friar, he studied at the International Seraphic College, the Pontifical Gregorian University, and the Pontifical University of St. Bonaventure, earning doctorates in both phi-losophy and theology. During World War II, Kolbe provided shelter to refu-gees from Poland, hiding thousands from Nazi persecution in his friary in *Niepokalanów.* On February 17, 1941, he was arrested by the German Ge-stapo and imprisoned in the Pawiak prison and then transferred to Auschwitz as prisoner 16670.

In January 1983, Aleksy Kucharski, a fellow prisoner at Auschwitz, shared his memories of Kolbe at the La Sierra Seventh-day Adventist Church in California:

At the time of [Kolbe's] arrival I did not know that he was a priest who had served as a missionary in Japan and as editor of the periodical *Knight of the Immaculate*. To me he was just another prisoner.

Soon, however, the priest's unflagging efforts to be of help to other prisoners caught my attention. His exceptional sensitivity toward others made me wonder who he was. Then one day we were assigned to the same work detail, hauling gravel in wheelbarrows to pave the roads inside the camp. Kolbe filled the barrows, and I pushed them to the road.

As we worked we talked, and I soon realized that Kolbe was not in a condition to do such rigorous physical labor. Having been a physical fitness instructor for the Polish Army, I found the work relatively easy, so I tried to ease his load as best I could.

Conditions in the camp were subhuman. Adequate food was not provided, the water was not pure, and proper sanitary procedures were not followed.[3]

Still, in the squalor of unthinkable suffering, Kolbe was, in the words of fellow inmate, Jerzy Bielecki, "a powerful shaft of light in the darkness of the camp."[4]

The story is told of the time Kolbe stumbled under the heavy load of wood. He was beaten within a strike of his life and dumped in the camp hospital. A Polish doctor, Rudolf Diem, recalls how Kolbe would share his meager rations of food. "You are young," he would say as he surrendered his watery soup to another patient. "You must survive."

Teetering on the edge of death, weighing less than one hundred pounds, Kolbe could have slept on a hospital bed. " 'But he insisted on a wooden bunk with a straw mattress,' recalls Dr. Diem. 'He wanted to leave the bed to someone whose lot was worse than his.' "[5]

Shortly after Kolbe's discharge from the camp hospital, a prisoner escaped during labor duty. The siren sounded. Search parties hunted the fugitive. The POWs were reminded that if the escapee was not found within twenty-four hours, ten of the six hundred men in Kolbe's Block 14 would be randomly selected and then tortured to death as retribution.

The prisoners of Block 14 were corralled for morning roll call. They stood all day in the scorching sun, awaiting death for ten unlucky victims. At 6:00 P.M., the camp commander, Colonel Fritsch, announced that the runaway had not been found. He would select ten prisoners to pay for the crime; they would be escorted to Block 13, where they would languish until they died of starvation.

Moving through the quadrangle of "living skeletons," the officer randomly stopped to point.[6] "You!" he'd bark. Guards would then grab the condemned captive.

One Polish soldier, cursed to die, was Francis Gajowniczek. When ripped from the ranks, he exclaimed, "Oh, my poor wife, my poor children. I shall never see them again."

As the ten men were removed from the ranks to go to death row, another prisoner stepped forward. It was Father Kolbe.

> "What does that Polish pig think he's doing?" Fritsch shouted. But the priest kept coming, unsteady, face white as death, ignoring the raised weapons of the guards. Finally, he spoke: "May it please the *Lagerführer*, I want to take the place of one of these prisoners." He pointed to Gajowniczek. "That one."
>
> Fritsch glared at the emaciated apparition before him, "Are you crazy?" the German snapped.
>
> "No," the priest replied. "But I am alone in the world. That man has a family to live for. Please."
>
> "What are you? What's your job?"
>
> "I am a Catholic priest."[7]

The prisoners watched in stunned disbelief. Finally, Fritsch shocked everyone with a curt reply, "Accepted."

Mieczyslaw Koscielniak, a commercial artist who witnessed the harrowing ordeal, later reflected, "We couldn't understand it. . . . Why would a man do such a thing? Who was he anyway, that priest?"[8]

As surreal as it was, Father Kolbe joined the ranks of the condemned. He volunteered to lie naked on the concrete floor of Block 13 with fellow sufferers who, over the course of the next two weeks, would inevitably slide into delirium then death. All the while Kolbe would comfort them with assurances that God had not forsaken them.

Bruno Borgowiec, one of the few Poles assigned to assist in the starvation bunker, recounts the details of Kolbe's death:

> The ten condemned to death went through terrible days. From the underground cell in which they were shut up there continually arose the echo of prayers and canticles. The man in charge of emptying the buckets of urine found them always empty. Thirst drove the prisoners to drink the contents. Since they had grown very weak, prayers were now only whispered. At every inspection, when almost all the others were now lying on the floor, Father Kolbe was seen kneeling or standing in the centre as he looked cheerfully in the face of the SS men.
>
> Father Kolbe never asked for anything and did not complain, rather he encouraged the others, saying that the fugitive might be found and then they would all be freed. One of the SS guards remarked: *This priest is really a great man. We have never seen anyone like him.*

Two weeks passed in this way. Meanwhile one after another they died, until only Father Kolbe was left. This the authorities felt was too long. The cell was needed for new victims. So one day they brought in the head of the sick-quarters, a German named Bock, who gave Father Kolbe an injection of carbolic acid in the vein of his left arm. Father Kolbe, with a prayer on his lips, himself gave his arm to the executioner. Unable to watch this I left under the pretext of work to be done. Immediately after the SS men had left I returned to the cell, where I found Father Kolbe leaning in a sitting position against the back wall with his eyes open and his head drooping sideways. His face was calm and radiant.[9]

Back in Block 14, Gajowniczek struggled to come to grips with Kolbe's sacrifice on his behalf. He cried uncontrollably and refused to eat. A fellow inmate reasoned with him, "Take hold of yourself," he hissed. "Is the priest to die for nothing?" Gajowniczek determined that Kolbe's gift would not be in vain. He would survive. He must live.[10]

Gajowniczek did outlive the death camp. He died on March 13, 1995, at Brzeg in Poland, at the age of ninety-five. After the war, Gajowniczek returned to his hometown with the dream of being reunited with his family. He found his wife—but his two sons had been killed during the war.[11]

Gajowniczek, of course, would never forget the sacrifice of the ragged monk, his starving savior. Every year on August 14, the anniversary of Kolbe's death, he made a pilgrimage to Auschwitz. For the next fifty-three years, Gajowniczek paid homage to the man who died for him.

"Father Maximilian went voluntarily to this most evil place ever erected by man, conquering its confines with a heart full of love," writes Antonio Ricciardi in his biography of Kolbe. "Thus hatred was replaced by love, injury by pardon, cursing by prayer. . . . With his self-immolation, Father Kolbe, who had become a mere number, won the hardest of all victories—the victory of love, which forgives and pardons."[12]

~⌖~

The River and Jordan

WHILE IN THE THICK OF COMPILING THESE STORIES, MY WIFE TOLD ME THE *inspiring report she saw on TV of Jordan Rice. A quick search on Google, and I was scrolling through hundreds of hits that told this amazing story of sacrifice. A couple of weeks after the flood, I was in Toowoomba, Australia. What a sobering experience it was to stand in the very spot where it happened. I imagined the terror, the angry river ripping through the town, the desperate fear, and the unthinkable selflessness.*

On January 10, 2011, Beau Nunn was perched on his roof, watching an empty Cessna plane rush by. The fifty-one-year-old country singer helplessly observed the "inland tsunami" that carved canyons into the land around him, funneling houses, cars, and even concrete water tanks in its wake.

"It was like being on a houseboat dodging missiles," he said. "If anyone of those things would have hit our house, we would have been in the drink. We just sat there watching and freaking."[1]

Beau sat in the epicenter of what Anna Bligh, Queensland's premier, called "the worst natural disaster in our history."[2] Dozens dead. Thousands displaced. And water drenching an area larger than France and Germany. No wonder many dubbed it a "disaster of biblical proportions."[3]

It often happens in disasters of this magnitude that an unlikely hero emerges as the face of tragedy. In the case of Australia's deadly floods, the world embraced a thirteen-year-old boy named Jordan Rice.

Jordan was naturally reserved and deeply devoted to his family. His brother Kyle, sixteen, describes Jordan in this way: "He was really shy with everyone else, wouldn't say a word to them. But when it came to the rest of his family, well, he'd do anything for them."[4]

On that fateful Monday, Jordan joined his forty-three-year-old mother, Donna Rice, and his ten-year-old brother, Blake, on a shopping trip to buy his school uniform. On the way home from shopping, their white Mercedes stalled in shallow floodwaters.

Under normal circumstances, splashing through a large puddle of water is great fun for a kid; the water sprays up in a wave that leaves one feeling like Moses escorting the Israelites through the Red Sea. But these were not normal circumstances. Panic seized Donna as she tried in vain to restart her car.

Flash floodwaters were rising—quickly.

Frantically, Donna called emergency services. "Stay in the car," she was told. But the water kept rising, forcing Donna and her boys to the roof of her vehicle.

That's when a thirty-seven-year-old businessman named Warren McErlean, along with another man known only as Chris, jumped into action. Securing themselves with ropes, they ventured into the furious current of water toward the distressed victims.

When help arrived, Jordan insisted that his little brother be rescued first. "Save my brother," he shouted.

"Courage kicked in, and he would rather his little brother would live," Jordan's brother Kyle reported to the Australian newspaper.[5]

"I'll never forget watching the family debate what order they should be saved," said Warren. "Jordan was arguing because he wanted the younger boy to go first."[6]

But there was no time to argue. The rope was fraying and the water was rising. The rescuer tied Blake to a rope and carried him to land.

Having delivered Blake to safety, Warren and Chris tried to return to the stranded mother and son. When the rope snapped, however, Chris was thrown into the air but managed to grab onto another post when he landed. "[Chris] looked at me and we knew it was over," Warren said.[7]

Jordan and Donna were swept off the car's roof—swallowed by the churning torrent of brown water. Momentarily, "they both clung to a tree, and when Jordan couldn't hang on any more, Donna let go and tried to save him," said cement worker John Tyson, Jordan's father and Donna's partner. "The last thing she did was to try to save [our] son."[8]

John would spend the night of his forty-sixth birthday visiting his son and partner in the mortuary. John did not want to go and identify the bodies, but Blake insisted.

"I think it gave him something to cling to," John said. "If looking at your dead mum and brother is something to cling to. It was the first time I have cried since I was 13. There I was on my birthday. Some . . . present, identifying my missus and kid, and looking at Jordan's broken finger sticking out.

"It is so hard but I have my other boys and I have to stay strong for them."[9]

John further reflected, "Jordan gave his life to save his brother.

"He has touched the whole world and left a legacy to show human goodness.

"I always told Jordan to do the best he could and he did this amazing thing for Blake. Donna and I brought up the kids to be kind to other people."[10]

Being kind is one thing. Giving your life so your brother can live is something altogether different. No wonder Jordan Rice is being heralded around the world as a "true hero" and "an angel." I would describe Jordan as the closest thing we see on this earth to our Savior.

Jordan's heroism is celebrated through thousands of posts on Facebook. The tributes are many:

- Such a traumatic event for a ten-year-old. His and his dad's life will never be the same. I'm positive there is a whole lot of loving going on between the friends and family affected. This story was on the main Yahoo page; I read it this morning and it stuck with me all day. It's incredibly tragic but incredibly inspiring at the same time.
- Rest in peace, big Man. He remains in our memories as a hero, a true brother, a Man.
- Actions truly do speak louder than words. You don't see many young kids these days thinking of others, other than themselves. You're a true Aussie hero, mate. What you did was incredible; I still shed a tear every time I hear your story. I'm proud to call myself Australian. RIP buddy ♥ from Dalby xox.
- What an incredible young man. Our world is that much poorer for your loss, and your selfless actions speak volumes about bravery and sacrifice.
- Your name will remain in my family's heart forever, Jordan. My son will tell his son the story of Jordan and his beautiful mother, Donna.

"He would have shunned the fame if he were living," says his dad.

"He was an introverted boy and he would have shied away from all that. . . . But he should get some kudos. He gave his life to save his brother. He deserves his time to shine."[11]

"The greatest love a person can show is to die for his friends" (John 15:13, NCV).

His Forgiving Heart

"Father, forgive them, for they do not know what they are doing."
—Luke 23:34

Ride, Ride Through the Day

T HE TALE OF JACQUES CELLIERS IS A FAVORITE THAT I INCLUDED IN MY BOOK Pilgrim's Problems. *Now, it just doesn't feel right to leave it out of this compilation of stories about sacrifice.*

Let's begin with the tragic end of his story. Jacques Celliers died in Java, at a prisoner-of-war camp just before peace was declared in 1945. In a gross violation of camp rules, an irate Japanese officer was poised to execute one of the prisoners. In an attempt to save his friend's life, Celliers approached the Japanese officer and kissed him on both cheeks like a French general honoring a soldier after a decoration for valor. The shock and humiliation of this gesture so infuriated the officer that it was Celliers who was killed instead.

The manner of Celliers's death was disturbingly inhumane. The prisoners were ordered to dig a hole in the center of the compound. Celliers was then escorted out of his cell and dumped into the hole. His comrades were then forced to fill the hole, leaving exposed only Celliers's bruised head, chin, and neck. Two days later, his strikingly handsome face and sun-bleached hair slumped into the dirt.

Before he died, however, Celliers recorded his life story. Wrapping his journal in a piece of military ground cloth, he buried it in the cell floor, where it was later discovered. His story begins with these sobering words:

> I had a brother once and I betrayed him. The betrayal in itself was so slight that most people would find "betrayal" too exaggerated a word, and think me morbidly sensitive for so naming it. Yet as one recognizes the nature of the seed from the tree, the tree by its fruit, and the fruit from the taste on the tongue, so I know the betrayal from its consequences and the tyrannical flavour it left behind it in my emotions.[1]

Celliers was the oldest of four children—two girls, two boys. Both of the girls died in the typhoid epidemic that ravaged their homeland of South Africa. Thus only the two boys remained.

There could not be a sharper contrast between Celliers and his brother. Celliers was tall, strong, and incredibly handsome. His skin was flawless, his face punctuated by dark blue eyes and crowned in flowing blond hair. Stories flourished of times when Celliers would walk into a crowded room and people would cease their conversations to stare. Celliers was a natural leader with a keen intellect, a sharp tongue, and natural athletic abilities. He fostered a deep love for the outdoors, often roaming the wild jungles and plains of South Africa to observe the majestic animals. It was clear that destiny had smiled upon him at birth.

His brother, seven years his junior, was different in every possible way. He was short, awkward, poor at academics, and as athletic as a platypus on ice skates. His hair was thick and dark and grew menacingly low onto his forehead. His skin was Mediterranean olive. His eyes burned of an intense radiant blackness, which prompted Celliers to later recount, "I could never look in them without feeling curiously disturbed and uncomfortable." Celliers also added, "I wish I could deal more firmly with this subtle discomfort but I cannot. I only know it was there from the beginning and as far back as I can remember it expressed itself from time to time in an involuntary feeling of irritation which, no matter how unreasonable and unfair, no matter what precautions I took to the contrary, would break out impatiently from me."[2] He cared little for animals but loved to work in dirt. Whatever he planted seemed to grow.

There was one area, however, where genetics had flipped the coin. Celliers was tone deaf. In contrast, from an early age the younger brother had a clear, unhesitating soprano voice that developed as he grew older into a manly and perfectly pure tenor instrument. He even composed music that moved the deepest emotions. Celliers recalled a signature tune that always stirred his innermost, unrealized longings. The lyrics went like this:

> Ride, ride through the day,
> Ride through the moonlight
> Ride, ride through the night.
> For far in the distance burns the fire
> For someone who has waited long.

But there was one irregularity, more than any other that blighted that brother's life. Between his shoulders grew a razor-edged hump. It brought him such shame that he never spoke of it. His mother padded his jackets to try to camouflage that awful projection. Although it was actually nothing more than a slight deformity, it grew like a mountain in his mind, making him a recluse from the world. In his journal, Celliers recounts, "We never referred to it by name. We always designated it by an atmospheric blank in our sentences. For instance, I would say, 'But if you do go swimming there wouldn't they see . . . blank.' Or he to me: 'D'you think if I wore that linen jacket it would . . . blank . . . you know?' "[3]

That hump is what prompted Celliers to begin his story with the confession, "I had a brother once and I betrayed him." The torment of his failure dated back to his senior year in school. Halfway through that last year, Celliers's parents decided to send his brother to join him at boarding school. Although the brother needed another year at the village school, the parents thought it would be easier for him if he had an older brother to guide his awkward paces that first year away from home.

The year had gone well for Celliers. He recalls,

> I was in the first eleven, captained the first fifteen, won the Victor Lodo-rum medal at the annual inter-school athletics, and was first in my final form. . . . Both masters and boys confidently predicted that at the close of the year I would be awarded the most coveted prize of the school, that for the best all-round man of the year. It was to this brilliant and crowded stage that I returned from vacation with my strange brother at my side.[4]

Little did Celliers anticipate how quickly the students would spread the news of this "strange fish" that had been thrown up on the school beach when his brother arrived. Celliers recalls, "From the very first evening, the start was not encouraging. First impressions are important to the young and never more important than when there are initiation rites to perform."[5]

Celliers had discussed the initiation proceedings on numerous occasions with his brother. He told him about running the gauntlet in pajamas with the students standing in two rows flicking wet towels plaited to a fine lashlike point; about waking up at night and finding a boy sitting with pillows on his head while others put a slip-knot of a fishing line round his toes and pulled at them until they bled in a perfect circle; about being made to measure the distance from school to town with his toothbrush on the holidays. As Celliers described the type of initiations that could transpire, nothing seemed to dismay the brother. The only thing he truly feared was his back being exposed and ridiculed.

On numerous occasions, Celliers responded to his brother's big question: "You don't suppose they would make fun of . . . you know . . . will they?"

"Of course not," Celliers replied. "You're going to a decent school, not a calf pen."

In spite of Celliers emphatic answer, his brother worried constantly about being exposed. Over and over Celliers heard the same question: "They won't—will they?"

One evening Celliers snapped. "Won't what? Never ask me again! Do you understand?"

The question was on his brother's lips again as Celliers conducted rounds of the dormitories the night before the initiations were to take place. Noticing his brother's apprehension, Celliers turned quickly away and bade him a curt "Good night" before slamming the door.

After rounds, Celliers joined the head monitors of the other three dorms in the office of the captain of the school. Following the usual pleasantries, the captain said, "We need to talk about the little matter of tomorrow's initiation. I take it you've all interviewed the newcomers in your houses. Have you any youngster you think should be excused?"

"Yes," the young man next to Celliers replied. "I have a boy with a weak heart who brought a doctor's certificate."

"No problem," the captain replied.

"Yes," said another, "I have a boy who is blind as a bat. He'd probably better be excused all the physical rites though there was no reason why he shouldn't be available for the rest of the fun."

After a couple of other students were mentioned, the captain looked keenly at Celliers. "No one?" the captain asked.

"No," Celliers said.

"You've got a young brother in your house, haven't you?" the captain asked.

"I have."

"What about him?"

"Well, what about him?" Celliers sparred.

"I was merely wondering if he was all right—"

"Of course he's all right." Celliers's answer was vehement; still the captain persisted. "Forgive me, old chap," he said. "I don't want to badger you. If you say he's all right, we all accept it. But, knowing you, we realized the last thing you'd ask for would be special dispensation for a relative. So if you've any reason for wanting your brother excused tomorrow, we'd none of us think of it as favoritism."

Spontaneous applause circled the table. But Celliers insisted, "Awfully decent of you, but there's no reason, honestly."

The following day after classes, Celliers hid in the distance as he spied on his brother standing by the door of the senior science laboratory. He stood tentative, as he always did when possessed by only one thought.

Suddenly a stampede of unruly students appeared. They hoisted the Celliers kid on their shoulders and started chanting, "Why was he born so beautiful? Why was he born at all?" The mob grew rowdier and rowdier until one of the bigger boys shouted, "Chaps, this newcomer has got to do something for our entertainment. What shall it be?"

"Make him sing," a voice from the mob replied.

"Right!" the student punched him with a fist on the shoulder and demanded, "Come on, Greenie, you've had your orders. Sing, blast you, sing!"

Celliers remembers it like this:

Music as I have told you was peculiarly my brother's own idiom. With the prospect of singing, even in such circumstances, his courage appeared to come back. He obeyed at once and began to sing:

> "Ride, ride through the day,
> Ride through the moonlight
> Ride, ride through the night.
> For far . . ."

The opening notes were perhaps a trifle uncertain but before the end of the first line his gift for music confidently took over. By the second line his little tune sounded well and truly launched. But he didn't realize, poor devil, that the very faultlessness of his performance was the worst thing that could have happened. . . . The boys, quick to feel that the clear voice singing with such unusual authority was cheating the design of its ritual uttered an extraordinary howl of disapproval.[6]

The gang began to press toward a long, deep horse trough chanting, "Greenie's a liar and a cheat, he can't sing a note. Greenie's a fraud: drown him, drown him in the moat!"

Celliers remembers what happened next:

> For a moment my brother's white face remained outlined against the afternoon fire flaming along the red-brick quadrangle wall, his eyes ceaselessly searching the screaming, whistling mob of schoolboys. Then he vanished like the last shred of sail of a doomed ship into a grasping sea. . . .
>
> I could not see what was happening. My experience told me that my brother was being ducked vigorously in the troughs as we had all been before him. I knew the "drown" in the chant really meant "duck." All the same I was extremely nervous. I watched the struggle and tumult of yelling heads and shoulders by the water-trough, wondering whether it would never end.[7]

Instantly, the crowd went motionless and silent. An arm shot up holding a shirt and behind it a naked torso.

"Look chaps!" a voice rang out with a curious reflection. "Greenie has a humpback!"

For a moment there was silence as the boys stared at the dripping wet hump. Then they exploded with laughter, twisting and turning in hysterics.

In that moment of terror, a teacher burst onto the scene and squelched the madness. But peace came too late and at too high of a cost. That young, vulnerable, awkward boy was scarred for life. His ugly scar revealed, he soon dropped out of school.

Celliers remembered and lamented in his prison cell, "I had a brother once and I betrayed him." Celliers felt overwhelmed by his betrayal. The brothers rarely spoke again after the incident. A door on brotherhood had been slammed so tightly shut that neither of the two boys could pry it open.

The young brother went home to his garden and solitude and never sang another note. Celliers graduated and became a successful lawyer, but his heart was empty.

At the outbreak of World War II, Celliers was one of the first to volunteer. Although he was recruited for an administrative post in the adjutant-general's department, Celliers insisted that he be commissioned in the infantry instead. Getting his wish, he was soon sent with the first division of infantry to the battlefields of North Africa. There, the great need was for a special patrol to capture enemy soldiers to provide them information. Celliers volunteered to carry out this dangerous mission and penetrate deep behind enemy lines. In this military maneuver, Celliers found his niche. Coupled with his lifetime's experience in stalking game in his native land, Celliers was uniquely gifted for this task, thus ensuring success. He describes it like this:

> I got better and better at killing. In particular I was so good at the kind of raid I have described that I was taken away from my battalion and set to plan and lead raids further and deeper behind the enemy lines. I came back each time impatient of offers of leave and rest, asking only to be kept active and employed. I volunteered for every difficult and hazardous operation. . . . I gave myself no time for anything except war, hoping thereby to escape from my shadows, but they were too adroit for me.[8]

Next, Celliers was sent on a special mission to Palestine. He was stationed at a monastery called Imwash, one of the traditional sites of the ascension of Christ. The monks had vacated the space only days before their arrival, leaving fresh smells of frankincense and myrrh hanging about the cool corridors and gray stone halls.

Almost immediately, Celliers fell ill with malaria. In the past he had recovered quite quickly, but on this occasion the fever wouldn't break. With the help of his batman (a British officer's orderly), Celliers was moved out of the monastery into the open air under the canopy of clouds and stars that he loved so much. There he could be closer to the healing powers of nature.

Being outdoors, as it turned out, only prompted more bouts of delirium. Looking toward the holy shrine that marked the spot where tradition claims that Jesus ascended, Celliers believed he saw Jesus with the disciples. And he heard someone say in his hallucination, "Judas is dead! Judas is dead!"

Celliers saw himself, as it were, approaching Jesus and saying, "There are many rumors in Jerusalem and Rome that are not true. See, I am Judas . . . I am alive and I am here."

Celliers believed Jesus to take both his hands and help his fever-riddled body to its feet. Then, looking upward, Jesus exclaimed, "Thank You, Father. Now at last we can both be free."

"But I'm not free," Celliers protested. "I had a brother once and I betrayed him—"

"Go to your brother," Jesus replied, "and make your peace with him even as I have had to do with my need of you."

In that moment the fever broke, and sweat poured out like a tropical rain. Celliers determined to visit his brother at any cost, for he would not carry the lie of his betrayal with him to death.

Before breakfast the next day, Celliers summoned a doctor from Jerusalem and secured a month's convalescent leave. Though everyone thought it impossible, Celliers then managed to get from Palestine to Egypt and from Egypt to South Africa, with the help of old friends in the South African Air Force.

While driving to his brother's home, Celliers noticed how parched the land was. There was no grass left on the veldt, and the scrub was twisted and burnt black in the sun's fire; sheep and cows were so lean that their ribs and bones seemed about to pierce their taut skins. Vultures circled continually overhead. The smell of death was everywhere.

Arriving at his brother's home, Celliers approached the front door. Before he could knock, his brother's wife came out. Through a hardened expression she managed to utter a semblance of a greeting. "Well, this is a surprise. Come in and I'll call your brother. He'll be amazed to see you!" And then she asked, "Why didn't you send us word you were coming?"

"That's a long story," Celliers said, "and I can explain later. But where is he? I'll go and find him."

"Then I'll go on seeing to the dinner," she said. "He's in the garden at the back, giving the last of our water to the trees and vegetables. We've had a terrible time, as you've noticed I expect. No rain for a year. Sheep and cattle dying and all this lovely garden is practically dead." She glanced at Celliers as if he'd been off on vacation rather than fighting a bloody war.

Celliers walked to the back of the house and saw his brother a short distance away, bent over a plant. The blighting hump was even more pronounced in middle age.

In a few strides, they were face to face. In his brother's dark eyes, Celliers saw a life imprisoned from a moment far back in time. *"Ouboet,"* he said to his brother, using this Afrikaans term of endearment. "It's good to see you again, *Ouboet*—and still growing things."

The younger brother stammered. *"Ouboet,* um, I wish I'd known, ah, you were coming. I'd have liked to be there to meet you. But come on up to the house. You must be tired. Can you stay long?"

"No," Celliers explained quickly, "in a sense, I've no right to be here at all. It's taken me a fortnight to get here, and I'll be lucky to be back on the front in time if I'm not to get into serious trouble. So I'm going back in a few hours to catch the night train north. I've been hitchhiking my way by air down here. I've come here just to see you."

"Really, *Ouboet?*" he said in disbelief. "Is that really so?"

"I've come all this distance to you because of my great wrong. Of all my failures in life, not one has plagued me more than the time I betrayed you. I am here to ask your forgiveness."

"Oh, but surely, *Ouboet,*" he started to protest.

Begging him to listen, Celliers went on to recount in stark detail the events of that late afternoon when he had betrayed his brother. Pained, dark eyes locked with troubled blue eyes, and in a broken voice the kid brother managed to say, "You mean you came all the way from Palestine to tell me this? You took the only leave you've ever had from the war to come and tell me this?"

Celliers nodded, too broken up to speak.

"*Ouboet,* you've done many fine things," the younger brother said, "but never a braver one than you've done today. At last we're free of it all, thanks to you." In that moment of love and forgiveness, the brothers' love was reborn.

Celliers dismissed himself to prepare for tea. As he reached the steps of the house, he heard a crystal-clear tenor voice, silent for decades, beginning to sing:

> Ride, ride through the day,
> Ride through the moonlight
> Ride, ride through the night.
> For far in the distance burns the fire
> For someone who has waited long.

For the first time, Celliers heard a second stanza to the song:

> I rode all through the day,
> I rode through the moonlight
> I rode all through the night.
> To the fire in the distance burning
> And beside the fire found
> He who had waited for so long.

As if by some celestial cue, thunder rumbled deep in the sky. A great army of clouds chased away the last strays of blue. The downpour of rain began to revive two shredded, separated lives. Physical rain, yes; but spiritual rain rejuvenated as well. On that day the rain of the Holy Spirit healed the scorched and stricken hearts.

~

A Father's Struggle to Forgive His Daughter's Murderer

By Darold Bigger

I*T'S ONE OF THE MOST POWERFUL AND MEMORABLE SERMONS I HAVE EVER HEARD. In 1997, at the Walla Walla College Seventh-day Adventist Church, my friend Dr. Darold Bigger shared his struggle of trying to forgive Anthony, the man who sexually assaulted and murdered his twenty-two-year-old daughter Shannon. For his crimes, Anthony received life in prison without the possibility of parole for the first-degree murder, plus life in prison for the "attempted sexual assault," and another twenty years for armed robbery. Even with the assurance that the perpetrator of such heinous crimes will die in prison, it is often the case that the victim's loved ones never escape their own prison of unforgiveness. They live in captivity to obsessive thoughts of revenge and anger. As this quotation attributed to Lewis B. Smedes states, "To forgive is to set a prisoner free and discover that the prisoner was you."*[1]

This is what makes Darold's story so compelling to me. He and his wife, Barbara, have amazing insights into the messy maze of forgiveness. (Look for their two forthcoming books, both of which share their story. Having attended their seminar, I can highly recommend them—even before they are published!) Because he experienced God's forgiveness, Darold testifies of the forgiveness he freely granted Anthony. Darold explains, "Accepting my own guilt and God's forgiveness of me took away the knot in my stomach and my clenched fists and jaw. Experiencing God's forgiveness produced forgiveness in me for Anthony. It was God's gift."

God has truly freed Darold from that jail of resentment. God erased the spirit of vengeance that can destroy one's soul. Again, from Lewis B. Smedes: "Vengeance is having a videotape planted in your soul that cannot be turned off. It plays the painful scene over and over inside your mind. . . . And each time it replays, you feel the clap of pain again."[2] *For Darold, God graciously reached down and shut off that old VCR.*

The following excerpt from that 1997 sermon puts skin on the miracle of forgiveness— God's forgiveness for us, and our forgiveness for others.

∾

During the last year, since Shannon's death, I have discovered some sobering things about myself and have experienced some exciting things about God.

This has been a year of exploring my vulnerabilities and weaknesses. April and May were especially difficult months when Shannon's killer, Anthony, requested the right to change his guilty plea to not guilty—hoping to get out of prison. I faced my feelings toward him then in a way I hadn't had to do before. I was depressed to find myself an angry, resentful man.

The apostle John writes, "Dear friends, let us love one another, for love comes from God. . . . If anyone says, 'I love God,' yet hates his brother, he is a liar. For anyone who does not love his brother, whom he has seen, cannot love God, whom he has not seen. And he has given us this command: Whoever loves God must also love his brother" (1 John 4:7–21).

And who is my brother? . . . My brother is any other member of God's creation. We are all children of God. Each man is my brother. But I faced the reality this spring that each man is not my friend. I faced the truth that I do not love my brother as I would like.

I'm not ready to face Anthony yet. Not personally. Not in a letter. Not even in an imaginary conversation in my mind. I just don't have the capacity to love him as any one of God's creation deserves to be treated. Please don't think that I am suggesting that he ought to be excused for his crime. I believe accountability is a part of the gospel as much as freedom and forgiveness are. I'm just not able to love him in spite of what he has done. Yet I feel that is what God calls me to do. So what does that say about me? It says that I am a sinful human being, the chief of sinners with a huge amount of growth to make before I become what God wants of me. I have had to face myself as one who does not wear well the trademark of God's people.

At the times when I recognize my inability to face Anthony and a number of other people, I find it most useful to not pay attention to them. I will not to concentrate on their slights. I choose to let go of the desire to endlessly describe how they should have done things differently. I find it most helpful to let go of all that and pay attention to the One who demonstrates what real love is all about—to get myself back to the Source of love.

Ellen White has some wonderful things to say about that transformation. In *Steps to Christ,* she describes how this took place for John himself, the one who relates so clearly the command Jesus gives us to love one another.

> Even John, the beloved disciple, the one who most fully reflected the likeness of the Saviour, did not naturally possess that loveliness of character. He was not only self-assertive and ambitious for honor, but impetuous, and resentful under injuries. But as the character of the Divine One was manifested to him, he saw his own deficiency and was humbled by the knowledge. The strength and patience, the power and tenderness, the majesty and meekness, that he beheld in the daily life of the Son of God, filled his soul with admiration and love. Day by day his heart was drawn

out toward Christ, until he lost sight of self in love for his Master. His resentful, ambitious temper was yielded to the molding power of Christ. The regenerating influence of the Holy Spirit renewed his heart. The power of the love of Christ wrought a transformation of character. This is the sure result of union with Jesus.[3]

That's what I want for myself. I long and hope for that.

During the week of August 2–7, 2010, I heard Darold and Barbara share their story once again, this time at the Lake Tahoe camp meeting. Here is another window of wisdom from Darold's presentation:

I am an Irishman. I hear stories of my great-grandfather, who had such a volatile temper—glimpses of which I experience in my own life and have seen in some relatives. My great-grandfather had such a violent temper that when a horse with which he was working one day offended him, he got down from the saddle and clobbered this horse's head with his fist, causing the horse to fall to its knees.

I always assumed that if anybody did anything to a member of my family, I would attack that person with fury. . . . But when we got the announcement of Shannon's death, and then a day or two later we were able to focus our anger on the perpetrator of this crime, I would have expected all those furious emotions to erupt in me. It was a surprise to me that it didn't happen. I have no good explanation for it, but I was not consumed with rage and revenge. I was extremely grateful. It was a gift of grace to me that I did not deserve, that I did not create myself. God prevented me from having to face that. . . . I suppose it was because of my deep and profound grief.

Some of you have asked us about our attitude toward Anthony. It was a very impersonal encounter early on. We did go back for his hearing and sentencing. . . . We chose not to make a public statement to the judge in court. Part of that was my own wish not to allow Anthony to know that he had any more influence in my life than he already had. . . . I knew as a result of my doctoral studies that one thing on which criminals thrive is power over other people. So for me to have let the man who stabbed and slashed Shannon to death know how miserable his crime had made me seemed that it would have given him some kind of power over me—and I didn't want to surrender that information. So we wrote out our statements and submitted them in private to the judge.

When it came to the time of all of those testimonies, Anthony had a handful of people on his side of the courtroom—his mother, a sibling or two. The rest of the courtroom was absolutely filled with Shannon's family and church friends.

Toward the end of the testimony, the state's attorney, Bob Dean, made a very passionate appeal to the judge. He reminded her of the horrific nature of this crime and closed his appeal with words close to these, "This man"—and he pointed to Anthony who had been almost emotionless during this entire hearing; he spent most of the time with his head down, looking at the table in front of him, not making eye contact with anyone. Robert Dean pointed at him and said, "This man deserves to spend the rest of his life in his own private hell." At that, Anthony looked up at the state's attorney and gave him the finger.

So we left court that day with a visual image in our mind, not of a repentant, remorseful, "this was a horrible mistake of mine" attitude, but of an angry, resentful person who did not want to take responsibility for what he had done. . . .

I was grateful in those early months that God shielded me from the rage and anger that I would have anticipated feeling. Anthony was safely put away. We were able to begin processing over the next several months our sense of losing Shannon. And then we got the phone call from the state's attorney general's office. Anthony had filed an appeal. He wanted to change his appeal to not guilty.

Even remembering that phone call tightens my jaw and puts a knot in my stomach. I was absolutely furious. This man, who had admitted stabbing and slashing Shannon to death, now wanted to get out of paying the consequences for what he had admitted he had done. I was enraged. . . .

And yet, in spite of who we are, God is ours. So for me, now, the symptoms—the anger, rage, the hurt, the holding on to grievances—are no longer the problem. They are simply *symptoms* of the problem. If God Himself really is the Source of love, and we experience that love as a transforming power in our lives when we accept it from Him, then the symptoms remind us that we have gotten away from the Source of love. I've got to quit worrying about the symptoms and focus on the solution—living in the One who sees us as the worst of sinners and yet loves us anyway.

❧

Gobbling up Forgiveness

A TEENAGE PRANK GONE WRONG. *AN INNOCENT VICTIM DONE WRONG. AND the stage is set for an amazing gesture of grace.*

~

Victoria Ruvolo was twenty seconds away from her home in Lake Ronkonkoma, New York. But she would spend the next month in a hospital in a medically induced coma. Nearly every bone in her face was shattered. She would live in a spiderweb of tubes hooked to machines coaxing life back into her ailing body.

On November 13, 2004, a group of unruly teenagers were out for a little fun. Compliments of a stolen credit card, they purchased a twenty-pound frozen turkey. For kicks, nineteen-year-old Ryan Cushing chucked the bird from the rear window of their speeding car, shattering Ruvolo's windshield "with such force that it bent her steering wheel" before flattening her face.[1]

Surgeons reconstructed her head using three titanium plates. They warned friends and family that the impact of the guided missile could likely result in permanent brain damage. For Ruvolo, life was hanging precariously on a scalpel's edge. But she survived the ordeal and attended the hearing for Ryan Cushing.

Dressed in a black pantsuit and accented by a gold cross, Ruvolo entered the courtroom. For the first time, Cushing could observe the mutilated canvas displaying his gruesome handiwork. Filled with shame, he apologized repeatedly.

Now put yourself in Ruvolo's seat. Think about the months of painstaking rehabilitation; the tears, the pain, the terror. And now this hooligan stands before you groveling with remorse. So what would you do? Take a gavel to his temple? Spit? Shout? Curse? Turn away in disgust? Flip *him* the bird?

Any of these reactions would be understandable, even defensible. But Ruvolo did something extraordinary. She forgave him and requested that his sentence be reduced. Cradling his head, stroking his face, and patting his back, she consoled him. "It's OK," she whispered. "It's OK. I just want you to make your life the best it can be."[2]

Ruvolo had previously requested that the judge consider a more lenient punishment than the twenty-five years in prison that would be the expected measure for Cushing's charge of first-degree assault and other serious offenses. Suffolk County district attorney, Thomas Spota, said he agreed to the plea bargain at Ruvolo's insistence.

Ruvolo read the following statement:

Despite all the fear and the pain, I have learned from this horrific experience, and I have much to be thankful for. . . . Each day when I wake up, I thank God simply because I am alive. I sincerely hope you have also learned from this awful experience, Ryan. There is no room for vengeance in my life, and I do not believe a long, hard prison term would do you, me, or society any good.[3]

At Ruvolo's insistence, the prosecutor gave Cushing a cushy bargain: six months in jail and five years' probation. Considering the likely alternative, this was a lucky break for the young man. No wonder Cushing commented to reporters about Ruvolo on his way out of the courthouse, "I love the woman. . . . She's a wonderful woman."[4]

" 'I felt like I had someone's life in my hands,' Ruvolo said. 'I had been through what I had to go through. I didn't want to see a life rot away in jail. I didn't see how that would help me move up and move forward.' "[5]

And so Cushing served his time in the Suffolk County jail and completed his probation. As part of his required community service, he worked with Ruvolo in a program called TASTE. In it, Ruvolo helps kids on probation by talking to them about the ideas behind the acronym:

Thinking errors
Anger management
Social skills
Talking
Empathy

The program is an outreach to young people like Cushing who have made mistakes. The program starts with Ruvolo's story—complete with graphic pictures of her damaged face. The program's founder and attorney, Robert Goldman, then tells about the attack and the forgiveness that followed.

When Ruvolo then stands to address the crowd, she is often met with gasps of surprise that the healing, both inside and out was so complete.

"She has embraced this, she has made the message part of who she is," said Goldman.[6]

For years Cushing was required to talk to the kids in the TASTE program.

Now, he does so voluntarily. "I keep going back on my own because I want to reach at least one kid a session in that room," he explains. Then the conversation usually steers back to Ruvolo. "She did a big thing. She did what a lot of people I know wouldn't have done. I owe her a lot."[7]

As for Ruvolo, she acknowledges that the whole ordeal has changed her—for the better. " 'I'm trying to help others, but I know for the rest of my life I'll be known as "The Turkey Lady," ' said Ruvolo with one of her frequent smiles. 'Could have been worse,' she said. 'He could have thrown a ham. I'd be Miss Piggy!' "[8]

~&

Love Thy Neighbor

REINHOLD NIEBUHR ONCE SAID, "FORGIVENESS IS THE FINAL FORM OF *love.*"[1] *Nowhere is this "final form" more potent than at the Cross. Luke tells us, "When they came to the place called the Skull, they crucified him there, along with the criminals—one on his right, the other on his left. Jesus said, 'Father, forgive them, for they do not know what they are doing' " (Luke 23:33, 34). Indeed, grace from the Cross offers the invitation to start new, whole, clean.*

Such is the invitation that Mary Johnson extended to Oshea Israel. It is a story of forgiveness. And the final form of love.

"Unforgiveness is like cancer," says Mary Johnson. "It will eat you from the inside out."[2] She ought to know. After all, for twelve years she battled stage IV of this deadly "cancer of unforgiveness." How could she ever forgive the boy who shot and killed her only son, Laramiun Byrd?

The tragedy occurred in February 1993, when sixteen-year-old Oshea Israel murdered Mrs. Johnson's son after a quarrel at a party in Minneapolis, Minnesota. Oshea, who was involved in drugs and gangs, was tried as an adult. He was sentenced to more than twenty-five years in prison and served seventeen before he was released.[3]

"My son was gone," Mrs. Johnson reflects. "I was angry and hated this boy, hated his mother.

"[The murder] was like a tsunami. Shock. Disbelief. Hatred. Anger. Hatred. Blame. Hatred."[4]

"None of us wants to admit that we hate someone," Lewis B. Smedes observes. "When we deny our hate we detour around the crisis of forgiveness. We suppress our spite, make adjustments, and make believe we are too good to be hateful."[5]

Smedes captures Mrs. Johnson's spirit. "I was a Christian woman that was full of hatred for Oshea," she said. "I wanted him to serve life in prison. I wanted them to take the key and throw it away. He was an animal. And he deserved to be locked up, caged, for the rest of his life. And I carried that hatred and bitterness for many, many, many years."[6]

Intellectually, Mrs. Johnson knew that as a Christian she had to forgive Oshea in order to be forgiven herself. "So I told him at the trial that I forgave him. And I didn't think it was lip service, but over the years I found out, yes, that's all it was, was lip service. I was doing what the Word says, but it was not really in my heart."[7]

Mrs. Johnson started a support group to assist moms whose children had been killed and whose children killed. Mrs. Johnson explained that hurt is hurt, regardless of which side of a murder you happen to be on. But with all the talk about forgiveness and healing of hurts and so on, Mrs. Johnson was still an angry, revengeful person. Her deep, unspoken feelings toward Oshea were seething vitriol.

Mrs. Johnson's breakthrough came when she read a poem titled "The Two Mothers." It tells of two mothers talking in heaven. One identifies herself as the mother of Jesus. The punch line of the poem comes at the end when the second mother reveals the identity of her son: "He was Judas Iscariot; I am his mother."

Mrs. Johnson recalls, "So I read it again, and after the second reading, I heard within myself, *I want mothers of murdered children, and mothers of children that have taken life to come together and heal together.*" Later she said, "Well, I laughed. And I thought, *You know what, that is totally impossible. That just cannot happen.* And I didn't want it to happen. But it is a possibility. This group is in existence today; it came into existence in 2006."[8]

Mrs. Johnson's support group blossomed into an organization called From Death to Life. Its mission is to support mothers who have lost children to homicide and encourages forgiveness between families of murderers and victims.

Mrs. Johnson soon realized, of course, that if her ministry of healing was to carry any credibility, she would first have to forgive Oshea—*really* forgive him. In raw terms, she would have to meet the killer face-to-face.

Oshea, however, was not as enthusiastic about meeting the mother of the kid he murdered. After all, he could not forgive himself for what he had done. "Of course my initial reaction was, 'No, it's not going to happen,'" he explains. "What for? What do I need to see her for? So she could cuss me out or call me names or vent on me? I'm not doing it. I didn't want to accept the responsibility or hold myself accountable at that point yet. So . . . to look in her face and look at what I've done. . . . 'Nah. I'll pass.'"[9]

Mrs. Johnson's request was denied.

Nine months later she tried again. This time, the caseworker pitching the idea to Oshea left him no choice. Because he was experiencing a genuine heart change himself, Oshea was amenable to the meeting—although he knew it would not be easy or comfortable. But if he was ever going to be a man, he reasoned, then he had no other alternative but to take responsibility.

Before visiting Oshea, Mrs. Johnson was required to attend four two-hour preparation meetings. Indeed, there is a discipline around the arts of forgiveness and reconciliation that is complicated and involved; it must be carefully prepared for and calculated.

When the meeting day came, Mrs. Johnson approached Oshea and said, "I don't know you; you don't know me, let's just get to know each other."[10]

For Oshea, Mrs. Johnson's introduction was disarming. "That just totally set me calm," he says.

> Because here it is, someone that was interested in knowing the other side of the story or getting to know me before they pass judgment. From that moment on, I went in there to trust the process to allow everything to take place the way it was supposed to without being resistant, without getting in the way as we tend to do sometimes in our lives. We tend to get in the way of our own progress and good things and blessings that happen, so I just decided to get out of the way, remove my ego, which is easing God out, and to let Him do the work.[11]

By the end of their meeting, the miracle of forgiveness shone like a brilliant sunrise in the colorless cell. "The meeting was so good, so great, that I really didn't want it to end," recounts Oshea,

> but [I] wanted it to end on a positive note. So as I was getting up to get ready to leave to be escorted out, I looked across the table at Mary and asked her if I could give her a hug. Because I just wanted to show her that I was being sincere and genuine. And she agreed, which surprised me. So as she walked around the table, and I walked around to greet her, and I gave her a hug, it was like everything . . . the floodgates just opened, and she started crying hysterically. I'm trying to hug her and hold her up, and mind you, I've been in prison for 12 years at this point around hardened criminals, a whole bunch of stuff, and right now is the scariest moment of my life. Like, *This lady is crying, what am I going to do? Somebody help me.*[12]

Oshea's desperate prayer was answered. Upon his release from prison in December 2009, Mrs. Johnson recruited some nuns in her neighborhood to throw a welcome-home party for Oshea. More than thirty people showed up—even though most of them did not know Oshea, they greeted him and pledged support as he adjusted to life outside of prison.

It was after the party that Mrs. Johnson's landlord asked her a bizarre question: Would she be open to Oshea living next door to her?

Mrs. Johnson dismissed the idea. She figured Oshea wouldn't want to live so close to her. But then her landlord explained that he had already talked to Oshea about it, and he was excited about it. So it happened that "a convicted murderer ended-up living a door jamb away from his victim's mother."[13]

Naturally, their journey continues to present challenges. Oshea says, " 'I haven't totally forgiven myself yet, I'm learning to forgive myself. And I'm still growing toward trying to forgive myself.'

"To that end, Oshea is now busy proving himself to himself. He works at a recycling plant by day and goes to college at night. He says he's determined to payback Mary's clemency by contributing to society."[14]

Together, they travel extensively, sharing their remarkable story of forgiveness and reconciliation. In a recent interview with National Public Radio on a program called *StoryCorps,* Oshea and Mrs. Johnson concluded their conversation with each other by saying this:

Ms. JOHNSON: Well, my natural son is no longer here. I didn't see him graduate. Now, you're going to college. I'll have the opportunity to see you graduate. I didn't see him get married. Hopefully, one day, I'll be able to experience that with you.

Mr. ISRAEL: Just to hear you say those things and to be in my life in the manner which you are, is my motivation. It motivates me to make sure that I stay on the right path. You still believe in me. And the fact that you can do it, despite how much pain I caused you—it's amazing.

Ms. JOHNSON: I know it's not an easy thing, you know, to be able to share our story together. Even with us sitting here looking at each other right now, I know it's not an easy thing. So I admire that you can do this.

Mr. ISRAEL: I love you, lady.

Ms. JOHNSON: I love you too, son.[15]

Healing Water

T HE NIGHT BEFORE CHRIST'S CRUCIFIXION, HE AND HIS DISCIPLES CELE-
brated the Passover in an upper room in Jerusalem. In the ancient world, proper
etiquette would be for a servant to wash the guests' feet. The disciples were well
versed in the protocol, and, in fact, the pitcher, basin, and towel had already been laid out.
But nobody moved to serve.

Nobody, that is, except Jesus. In His example, we find the heart of humility, confession, and repentance. It is the same spirit that birthed a church in Tübingen, Germany.

The small, university town of Tübingen, Germany, had a well-deserved reputation as a center of anti-Semitism. Dating back to 1477, Tübingen expelled all of its Jewish residents. For generations, hatred for all things Jewish was embedded into the DNA of this community. Blatant bigotry thrived, especially during World War II. Not surprisingly, many notorious Nazi war criminals came from Tübingen.

Then in 1987, the Tübingen Offensive Stadtmission church (TOS) was established. It is a Protestant, charismatic free church that embraces a spirit of forgiveness and reconciliation. The church building appropriately sits on top of railroad tracks that carried trains full of Jews to death camps in Poland and Germany.

Under the leadership of Pastor Jobst Bittner, more than 250 TOS members are working to erode the centuries-long history of racism by reaching out to their Jewish brothers and sisters. With the understanding that the sins of the fathers are visited to the children to the third and fourth generation (see Exodus 20:5), Pastor Bittner has modeled repentance. He continues to challenge his congregation to join in the prayer of remembrance for those who were tortured and slain for no other crime than being Jewish.

In 2007, TOS members organized the March of Life to commemorate Holocaust Remembrance Day. The event was an effort to promote healing. German Christians walked more than two hundred miles together along the same route of the famous 1945 death march from Bisingen to Dachau.

The *Jerusalem Post* reports, "The march by these German Christians was aimed at healing the wounds of the past in order to build relationships that will last into the future."[1]

The evening before the march, TOS church members gathered for a time of prayer and confession. Four members shared difficult and emotional stories of their own family members collaborating with the Nazi regime. One choir member, Barbel Pfeiffer, shared her recent discovery that her own grandfather was an SS guard who committed horrific crimes against the Jews.[2]

This time for healing culminated when several TOS members approached their Jewish guests with towels and basins in hand. Following the example of Jesus, they washed the feet of the Holocaust survivors. The Jewish guests, in turn, washed the feet of the confessors. Tears flowed freely. "Rose Price, survivor of six camps, including Dachau, embraced and comforted . . . the Germans."[3] Together, they experienced authentic communion.

The story of the TOS revival brings to mind another Man of Jewish descent stooping to wash feet. He, too, was afflicted and abused. And how did He respond? With revenge? Retaliation? Vengeance? He had every right to pursue such a course. Instead, He humbled Himself and bathed smelly feet. Here is what happened next:

> After washing their feet, he [Jesus] put on his robe again and sat down and asked, "Do you understand what I was doing? You call me 'Teacher' and 'Lord,' and you are right, because that's what I am. And since I, your Lord and Teacher, have washed your feet, you ought to wash each other's feet. I have given you an example to follow. Do as I have done to you. I tell you the truth, slaves are not greater than their master. Nor is the messenger more important than the one who sends the message. Now that you know these things, God will bless you for doing them" (John 13:12–17, NLT).

Ellen White explains,

> In washing the feet of His disciples, Christ gave evidence that He would do any service, however humble, that would make them heirs with Him of the eternal wealth of heaven's treasure. His disciples, in performing the same rite, pledge themselves in like manner to serve their brethren. Whenever this ordinance is rightly celebrated, the children of God are brought into a holy relationship, to help and bless each other.[4]

Is there a relationship in your life that cries for restoration? A father who abandoned you? A stepmom who insulted you? A child who hurt you? Are there people who come to mind that you need to forgive—even if you did nothing wrong?

Dr. Dean Ornish rightly observes, "Forgiveness does not condone or excuse someone from their actions in hurting you; rather, it helps empower and free you from the pain of chronic anger, separation, and isolation."[5]

Before reading the next chapter, maybe you need to make a visit. And don't forget the basin and towel.

ॐ

His Closing Challenge

*Whenever you eat this bread and drink this cup, you
proclaim the Lord's death until he comes.*
—1 Corinthians 11:26

Graceful Exchange

MANY OF THE STORIES ABOUT SELF-SACRIFICING LOVE ARE ADMITTEDLY *quite dark and foreboding, detailing the spirit of sacrifice often onto death. As a respite from such stories, I have included a parable here that paints a picture of God's grace in lighter, more impressionistic tones. I can't recall the preacher. I don't remember the church. I just can't forget the parable the preacher shared with his congregation. It's been more than twenty years since I heard it, but the story remains one of my favorite snapshots of grace.*

The second story in this chapter is admittedly a bit less cheery. Nonetheless, I believe it reinforces the parable by putting skin on the notion of grace as an exchange of our un-righteousness for His righteousness.

Remember those old-fashioned church picnics? The pastor would announce, "Let's all meet at Creekside Park tomorrow at one o'clock. Bring your own supper."

At the last minute, you decide to go. Scrounging through the refrigerator, you find some tired slices of bread, a rusty head of lettuce, just enough mayonnaise to scrape your knuckles getting at it, and a pile of veggie bologna. You slap together a sandwich and scurry to the park.

The afternoon involves tug-of-war, egg tosses, three-legged relays, and lots of other games you haven't played since third grade. Finally, the pastor calls everyone together and blesses the food. You disappear into the shadows and plop down on a rickety picnic table. There you slump, ready to bite into your sorry sandwich when out of the corner of your eye you see something that looks like a living Norman Rockwell painting.

Here comes a chubby little grandma with white hair. She's carrying a picnic basket the size of a Volkswagen Beetle. She comes to your picnic table and unfolds a red-and-white-checked gingham tablecloth right up to your elbow!

And there you sit clutching your veggie bologna sandwich.

She unpacks her feast. She's got blackberry cobbler, blueberry pie, hot dogs, potato salad, Doritos, Fig Newtons, roasted corn, Cracker Jacks, FriChik, soda pop, peaches, pears; it's a feast that defies the senses.

And there you sit, clutching your bologna sandwich.

Just then, she looks over at you and says, "What do you say we just throw it all together? I've got plenty of cobbler and corn and pie—and besides, I just love bologna sandwiches."

Jackpot! You are stunned by your good fortune. You came as a pauper, but you eat like a prince or a princess.

So God comes to you sitting on that rickety picnic table called life. He unfolds His white linen tablecloth right up to your elbow. He looks down at you clutching all of your bologna. Just last week you cheated on an exam. Just last night you compromised at your computer. Just this morning your mind feasted on vindictive thoughts. Your soul is stuffed with bologna, and you wonder whether God is big enough to forgive.

That's when God examines what you bring to the table and He says, "Why don't we just throw it all together? You need forgiveness? I've got more forgiveness than you could ever use in one lifetime."

You offer up your bologna, and you are no longer a pauper but a perfect child of God. You see, in that moment, there is an exchange: your sin for Christ's sinlessness; your guilt for His grace; your bologna for His FriChik.

Ellen G. White described the miracle in this way: "Christ was treated as we deserve, that we might be treated as He deserves. He was condemned for our sins, in which He had no share, that we might be justified by His righteousness, in which we had no share. He suffered the death which was ours, that we might receive the life which was His. 'With His stripes we are healed.' "[1]

Erwin Lutzer reminds us of this good news: "There is more grace in God's heart than there is sin in your past."[2] Yes, you may own a factory of smelly bologna. But your offenses against a holy God can never eclipse the boundary of His grace.

An act of love

In his autobiography *Doctor Pygmalion,* the world-renown plastic surgeon Dr. Maxwell Maltz shares the love story of Andrea and Catherine—an unlikely couple. Andrea was from Italy. He was poor. His father died when he was young, and the only family that remained was his brother and mother, who were both severely crippled. Catherine was a wealthy heiress from New York.

The couple met at a New York dance when Andrea came to America to take an engineering course. For both Catherine and Andrea, it was love at first sight. Soon, they were married.

The newlyweds settled into a spacious estate. Catherine set up two rooms on the opposite side of their house—one for Andrea's mom and one for his brother. "It must have seemed to them I'd deliberately put them as far away from Andrea and me in the house as I could," Catherine explained to Dr. Maltz. "Before he'd gone to America, Andrea had always slept in a room between his mother's and his brother's rooms and he told me it worried him to have them at the far side of the house in the wing opposite ours, since they were cripples and couldn't help themselves."[3]

Catherine would long regret the living arrangements that she had made. For in the middle of the summer, tragedy struck. Fire broke out in their home. Catherine described that fateful night:

> "Andrea leaped up from the bed, and went running out of our room the way he was, because from the sound of the scream he knew that if he wasn't there in the next second it would be too late.
>
> "If only the screaming had been coming from the room next to ours—but it wasn't, it was all the way at the other side of the house. Andrea's brother had managed to crawl into their mother's room to try to help her but the smoke must have suffocated him, because by the time Andrea got there both of them were dead."[4]

In his attempted rescue, Andrea's face was severely burned and disfigured. Ashamed of his appearance and reeling in guilt, he locked himself in a room, refusing access to everyone—including his bride.

For three years, Andrea slid deeper and deeper into despair. As a last resort, Catherine contacted Dr. Maltz. "Not to worry," he assured her, "I can restore his face."

Catherine explained that Andrea had always refused any medical treatment. "Andrea said it was the penalty he had to bear for the death of his mother and brother, that nothing must be done to interfere with the justice of God."[5]

Assuming he wouldn't change his mind, Catherine then made a strange request of Dr. Maltz: "I want you to disfigure my face so I can be like him! If I can share in his pain, then maybe he will let me back into his life."

Dr. Maltz tried to mask his horror at the request. He was so moved by this woman's love, however, that he went to visit her husband. Through a closed door he yelled, "I'd like to talk to you. Will you let me in?"[6]

Dr. Maltz writes,

> There was silence for a few minutes. Then he spoke in English. There wasn't much accent but the voice had a curiously flat sound.
>
> "Are you the American doctor? . . .
>
> "There isn't any reason for you to see me," the flat voice said. "There's nothing you can do for me."
>
> "I know," I agreed. "I just feel I should tell you what I am going to do for your wife."[7]

Dr. Maltz told Andrea of Catherine's request—what he called "a grotesque act of love."[8] This is the idea he tried to explain: She wants me to mutilate her face in order to make her face like yours. She hopes that you will then let her back into your life. That's how much she loves you.

There was a long silence.

"How?" Andrea gasped. "To have that done to *her* face? . . . Monstrous, wicked, obscene! She'd be committing—blasphemy!"

"Well, no," Dr. Maltz said. "I think you should say that she would be committing an act of love."

Andrea could no longer hold in the tears.

"Come on, Andrea," Dr. Maltz said gently. "I promised to take Catherine to the hospital, but let's take you instead. Or—let's all three go together"[9]

An even greater act of love

The story of Andrea and Catherine provides a snapshot of God's love. It is a selfless, sacrificing, painful love that God calls for us to demonstrate to one another. Jesus said, "I command you to love each other in the same way that I love you. And here is how to measure it—the greatest love is shown when people lay down their lives for their friends" (John 15:12, 13, NLT).

Jesus took on our face, our disfigurement. It could be called "a grotesque act of love." For there was no place He would not go in order to reach us. He went to a hay trough, homes of ill repute, the Garden of Gethsemane, and a bloody cross. The love He modeled knew no limits. He did this in order to afford us the treatment that He deserves.

Doesn't that kind of love make you want to respond? Don't you want to spread that kind of love to others? Jesus stands at the door of your heart and says, "Look! Here I stand at the door and knock. If you hear me calling and open the door, I will come in, and we will share a meal as friends" (Revelation 3:20, NLT).

Won't you let Him in? And then, won't you let Him out?

❧

Of Tebowing and Delaneying

T HE National Football League (NFL) is no stranger to scandal. *From the offensive gesture flipped by the singer M.I.A. during Super Bowl XLVI to murder charges against Ray Lewis following Super Bowl XXXIV and on to a library of driving under the influence charges, domestic violence convictions, drug busts, dog fights, gun shots, and sexual harassment gaffes, the league's task of image management is like pulling 24/7 public relations duty for Charlie Sheen.*

Enter Tim Tebow.

Now there is a face for the league that boasts of decency, integrity, and purity. This guy elevates the whole sport to heavenly heights. I mean, when your name is used in the common vernacular as a verb for praying, you know you're making an impact for good—and for God.

But four years before Tebow was born, there was another star in the NFL. Like Tebow, he was a devoted Christian. Sunday mornings you could often find him serving as an usher at Galilee Baptist Church in Haughton, Louisiana. Unlike Tebow, his name is not a household synonym for God *or* faith *or* Christian, *but his story is every bit as uplifting—perhaps more so. As* Tebowing *has come to mean bowing in devotion to God, I think* Delaneying *should grace our lexicon to mean "laying down one's life in ultimate devotion." This is the story of no ordinary Joe.*

Joe Delaney lived his Christian faith. Stories abound of his selfless acts of altruism. He once paid the funeral costs for a former teacher whose family could not afford a proper burial. Whenever he returned home to Haughton, Louisiana, he'd visit a lonely woman to mow her lawn. He'd hit the streets to distribute new shoes and clothes for neighborhood kids. And every day he'd try and stop by to visit an old man.[1]

Delaney put others before himself. Even at Christmastime, his wife, Carolyn, would ask, "Don't you want *nothing* for yourself?"

"Nah," he'd shrug. "You just take care of you and the girls."[2]

Joe and Carolyn did care for their three girls, Tamika, Crystal, and JoJo (for

Joanna). They enjoyed an enviable life—this, in part, because of Joe's successful career in the NFL.

Despite many naysayers (including his own dad), Delaney surprisingly excelled as a football player. Selected in the second round of the 1981 draft by the Kansas City Chiefs, he rushed for over eleven hundred yards, set four club records, and was named Rookie of the Year of the American Football Conference.[3] The following season was cut short by a strike, interrupting what was destined to be the second of many of Delaney's successful campaigns in the NFL. But Delaney would not return for a third season as the Chief's star running back.

On June 29, 1983, the twenty-four-year-old professional athlete was relaxing in the shade of a tree at Chennault Park in Monroe, Louisiana, when he heard kids screaming, "Help! Help!" In the park was a two-acre crater filled with water—the result of displaced dirt created by the construction of a nearby amusement ride. With no fence surrounding the water, three boys ventured in for a refreshing splash. They were two brothers, Harry and LeMarkits Holland, eleven and ten, respectively, and their cousin, Lancer Perkins, eleven. There was no way for them to know that four feet from the grassy shore the hole dropped twenty feet.

Lots of people saw what was happening, but no one moved—except Delaney. On his way into the water, a boy asked him, "Can you swim?"

"I can't swim good," Joe said, "but I've got to save those kids. If I don't come up, get somebody."

According to one online report, the youngest boy, LeMarkits, remembers sinking into the cold bottom, with water filling his lungs when a massive hand grabbed his shoulder and yanked him from the watery grave. There are also reports of doubt that LeMarkits's savior was Delaney.

On the twenty-year anniversary of the tragedy, ESPN produced a piece retelling the story. " 'It's hard,' said ESPN coordinating producer Glenn Jacobs, 'to separate the myth or the legend from what really happened.' " "There are differing accounts of whether it was really Delaney saving LeMarkits. No matter what happened, it doesn't change the basic fact that Delaney was a hero. He rushed into the water to save people."[4]

There is no question that Delaney tried to rescue the boys. But his heroic attempt would end in tragedy. This unlikely trio of young men would all drown together.

Delaney was buried on July 4.

"I'm going to miss you, Joe," Delaney's mother Eunice cried at his grave. "God knows, I'm going to miss you."[5]

On July 15, President Ronald Reagan honored Delaney with the Presidential Citizens Medal. Vice President George H. W. Bush shared this message from the president: "He made the ultimate sacrifice by placing the lives of three children above regard for his own safety. By the supreme example of courage and compassion, this brilliantly gifted young man left a spiritual legacy for his fellow Americans."[6]

"We've always looked upon Joe as being one of the most caring persons we ever met," reflects Delaney's sister Alma. "All of us in the Delaney clan, we do what we can to help the other person. But would I have dove in to that water, not being able to see? That goes through my mind. But Joe never thought of that." Alma pauses, reflecting on several losses in her life. "The Lord has embraced me throughout," she said, finally. Calling on Scripture, she mentions this text: "Greater love hath no man than to lay down his life for another."[7]

That verse captures Delaney's life—and death. Down a dirt road off Louisiana Highway 157, in the small town of Bellevue, just beyond the telephone pole marked 58, you'll find that scripture carved into his tombstone.

"Joe lived and died a hero," Monroe, Louisiana's, newspaper, the *News-Star* quoted Delaney's wife, Carolyn.[8]

Sports Illustrated columnist Rick Reilly provides a more recent quote from Carolyn:

> She thinks of her Joe every day. She can't help it. Their three daughters and four grandkids remind her of him constantly. There is a pause. "I never thought we wouldn't grow old together."
>
> She's only been on two dates since Joe died. Twenty years, two dates. "Why should I?" she says. "I just keep comparing them to Joe, and they can't stand up. Nobody in the world is like my Joe."[9]

Nobody? Well, perhaps there was one Man like her Joe—and her Joe is like this Man. Like Joe, Jesus ventured into the muddy waters of this planet to attempt a rescue of victims drowning in sin. He willingly gave His life to save you.

How will you respond?

❦

Chapter 23

The *Titanic's* Last Hero

By Moody Adams

O NE OF MY FAVORITE STORIES IS THIS ONE ABOUT JOHN HARPER. THE FULL *story is told in the book* The *Titanic's* Last Hero. *I was thrilled to meet the author, Moody Adams, who graciously and enthusiastically granted permission to reprint his work. He said, "I am just thrilled to further the story of this great soul winner." Without question, John Harper embodies the Christian ideal of sacrificing all.*

John Harper was born to a pair of solid Christian parents on May 29, 1872. It was on the last Sunday of March 1886, when he was thirteen years old, that he received Jesus as the Lord of his life. He never knew what it was to "sow his wild oats." He began to preach about four years later at the ripe old age of seventeen years old by going down to the streets of his village and pouring out his soul in earnest entreaty for men to be reconciled to God.

As John Harper's life unfolded, one thing was apparent . . . he was consumed by the Word of God. When asked by various ministers what his doctrine consisted of, he was known to reply, "The Word of God!" After five or six years of toiling on street corners preaching the gospel and working in the mill during the day, Harper was taken in by Pastor E. A. Carter of Baptist Pioneer Mission in London, England. This set Harper free to devote his whole time and energy to the work so dear to his heart.

Soon, John Harper started his own church in September of 1896 (now known as the Harper Memorial Church). This church, which John Harper had started with just twenty-five members, had grown to over five hundred members when he left thirteen years later. During this time he had gotten married, but was shortly thereafter widowed. However brief the marriage, God blessed John Harper with a beautiful little girl named Nana.

Ironically, John Harper almost drowned several times during his life. When he was two and a half years of age, he almost drowned when he fell into a well but was resuscitated by his mother. At the age of twenty-six, he was swept out to sea by a reverse current and barely survived, and at thirty-two he faced death on a leaking ship in the Mediterranean. Perhaps, God used these experiences to prepare this servant for what he would face next.

It was the night of April 14, 1912. The RMS *Titanic* sailed swiftly on the bitterly cold ocean waters heading unknowingly into the pages of history. On board this luxurious ocean liner were many rich and famous people. At the time of the ship's launch, it was the world's largest man-made moveable object. At 11:40 P.M. on that fateful night, an iceberg scraped the ship's starboard side, showering the decks with ice and ripping open six watertight compartments. The sea poured in.

On board the ship that night was John Harper and his much-beloved six-year-old daughter Nana. According to documented reports, as soon as it was apparent that the ship was going to sink, John Harper immediately took his daughter to a lifeboat. It is reasonable to assume that this widowed preacher could have easily gotten on board this boat to safety; however, it never seems to have crossed his mind. He bent down and kissed his precious little girl; looking into her eyes, he told her that she would see him again someday. The flares going off in the dark sky above reflected the tears on his face as he turned and headed toward the crowd of desperate humanity on the sinking ocean liner.

This Scotsman's selfless heroism is accentuated by the contrasting conduct of many fellow passengers on this death voyage. While Harper gave up his life jacket, an American banker managed to get a pet dog into a lifeboat, leaving 1,522 humans unaided. There was little of the "go-down-with-the-ship" spirit. Of the 712 saved, 189 were, in fact, men of the crew. Colonel John Jacob Astor tried to escape with his wife into a lifeboat and had to be stopped by Second Officer Charles Lightoller. Astor was the richest man in the world, but he was powerless to force his way into a measly little lifeboat. Daniel Buckley disguised himself as a woman in an effort to gain a place in a lifeboat. First-class passengers on the first lifeboat to be lowered refused to turn back to pick up people who were drowning, though there was space for many others to have been saved. Mrs. Rosa Abbott, the only woman to go down with the ship and survive, said a man tried to climb up on her back, forcing her down under the water and nearly drowning her.

Mr. Bruce Ismay, part owner of the *Titanic* and a managing director of the White Star Company and the man responsible for not putting [enough] lifeboats on board, became the most infamous seaman since Captain Bligh. He crawled into a lifeboat while hundreds of women remained on the dying ship. Captain Smith ordered his men to, "Do your best for the women and children, and look out for yourselves." At the same time John Harper was ordering men to do their best for the women and children and look out for *others*.

As the rear of the huge ship began to lurch upwards, it was reported that Harper was seen making his way up the deck yelling, "Women, children, and unsaved into the lifeboats!" It was only minutes later that the *Titanic* began to rumble deep within. Most people thought it was an explosion; actually the gargantuan ship was literally breaking in half. At this point, many people jumped off the decks and into the icy dark waters below. John Harper was one of these people.

That night 1,528 people went into the frigid waters. John Harper was seen swimming frantically to people in the water, leading them to Jesus before the hypothermia became fatal. Mr. Harper swam up to one young man who had climbed up on a piece of debris. He asked him between breaths, "Are you saved?" The young man replied that he was not.

Harper then tried to lead him to Christ only to have the young man, who was near shock, reply No. John Harper then took off his life jacket and threw it to the man and said, "Here then, you need this more than I do," and swam away to other people. A few minutes later Harper swam back to the young man and succeeded in leading him to salvation.

Of the 1,528 people who went into the water that night, six were rescued by the lifeboats. One of them was this young man on the debris. Four years later, at a survivors' meeting, this young man stood up and in tears recounted how John Harper had led him to Christ. Mr. Harper had tried to swim back to help other people, yet because of the intense cold, had grown too weak to swim. His last words before going under in the frigid waters were, "Believe on the name of the Lord Jesus and you will be saved."

Does Hollywood remember this man? No. Oh well, no matter. This servant of God did what he had to do. While other people were trying to buy their way onto the lifeboats and selfishly trying to save their own lives, John Harper gave up his life so that others could be saved.

"Greater love has no one than this: to lay down one's life for one's friends." John Harper was truly the hero of the *Titanic*![1]

✧

The Story Not to Be Shared

By C. Douglas Sterner

E MERGING FROM THE HORRORS OF WAR ARE SOME OF THE MOST TOUCHING *stories of extraordinary love and service. Richard Nott Antrim offers a good example. Thankfully, his story became public and now inspires all who hear it to live with the same spirit of sacrifice.*

∾

Brotherhood is more than biological; it is fraternal. It develops quickly among men in uniform, both in peacetime and during time of war, simply by virtue of the call to duty they share in common. There is a sense of family among men in uniform, a common bond to look out for one another. But how far will one brother go on behalf of another? The horrors of war often test the limits of that brotherhood.

Richard Nott Antrim became a part of a very special brotherhood when he graduated from the U.S. Naval Academy in 1931. Naval officers have always shared a kindred spirit. To the men who served under him in the years that followed, Antrim was a capable leader. As executive officer of the USS *Pope* when World War II began, he was a man of rank who inspired confidence. On March 1, 1942, disaster struck the men of the USS *Pope*. For the next three years the survivors would need more than a leader, they would need a "big brother." No one could have imagined how big would be the shoulders of Richard Nott Antrim, the stronger, older brother they would all need to see them through a crucible of unimaginable horrors.

Among the myriad of tales of courage and heroism that fill the annals of Medal of Honor history, the story of Richard Nott Antrim has always been one of the most inspiring. . . . It was a story, however, that could not rightly be told for many years. When Rear Admiral Antrim retired from the navy in April 1954, he settled with his family in the quiet community of Mountain Home, Arkansas, to run a small tour boat. In the community everyone knew him as "Dick," and that is how he wanted it. Tom Dearmore was editor of the local newspaper and one of Dick's friends. One day when Tom asked Dick about his Medal of

Honor action, the kindly man whose only concerns were for the welfare of his community pointed his finger at Tom and said, "I don't want it published—I don't want to ever read anything about it in your newspaper." Thirty years after Dick Antrim's death, Tom finally wrote the story saying, "He [Antrim] has been dead 30 years now and will not reproach me."

In preparing this story, I first sought the approval of Rear Admiral Antrim's family. I am especially indebted to Judy Antrim Laylon for her assistance in putting together this glimpse into history that needs to be told and retold, not to glorify the heroism of the humble hero who graced our world, but so that his example can inspire others to put the needs of others before themselves. Ms. Laylon wrote: "My father was a very modest man and probably wouldn't have contributed the information about his heroism, but I feel this generation who has not really experienced war needs to know about the people who came before them and what they did to preserve our freedom."

Richard Nott Antrim was born in Peru, Indiana, where he lived his early life with his mother, Mary, who was a local school teacher. Young Dick Antrim attended Peru public schools and found a good balance between education and athletics. Two years before his high school graduation in 1926, he was part of the squad that won the Wabash Valley Football Conference championship. From there he received an appointment to the U.S. Naval Academy at Annapolis, where he played varsity football for three years, graduating on June 4, 1931.

Two years later Dick and his young wife Mary Jean welcomed daughter Judy to the family. A second daughter, Nancy, was born two years later. In May 1937, the family was living at the Lakehurst Naval Station in New Jersey when the *Hindenburg* began its approach. Dick Antrim was on the mast to anchor the dirigible when tragedy struck. Standing on the porch of the Antrim home, Jean and four-year-old Judy watched in horror as fire rained down around the naval officers stationed below. It was a moment of horror that tried the soul of the Antrim family. "Two things went through my mind," Jean later wrote. "If Dick is alright he won't want me running around, he'll want me at home. The other, if any thing has happened I must be here to receive word, so I stuck my ground." Dick survived, but the strength of character that Jean Antrim exhibited that day would receive its greatest trial in years that lay ahead.

In December 1939, Naval Lieutenant Richard Nott Antrim was assigned to the USS *Pope* (DD-225), an aging but important part of the Asiatic fleet. Mary Jean and daughters Judy and Nancy had returned home to Peru, Indiana, while Dick was serving at sea. When the Japanese bombed Pearl Harbor on December 7, 1941, the seven- and nine-year-old girls knew it would be a long time before they saw Daddy again. They didn't realize, however, just how long it would be.

In the first eighty days after Pearl Harbor, the USS *Pope* served well in two major engagements, the Battle of Makassar Strait and the Battle of Badoeng Strait. The cool, effective leadership of the *Pope's* executive officer led Commander

Welford C. Blinn, the ship's commanding officer, to recommend Richard Antrim for "a decoration deemed appropriate . . . for the meritorious performance of his several duties before and throughout the action." Though eventually that recommendation resulted in the award of the Navy Cross to Lieutenant Antrim, before it would be awarded, his courage would be tried even more severely than it had been during those long hours of naval combat. It would be one of many recognitions eventually conferred on the humble hero from Peru.

During three and a half years of captivity as a prisoner of war, Lieutenant Antrim would prove to be not only courageous, but also ingenious. The citation for his subsequent Bronze Star award speaks for itself:

> For heroic service while a Japanese Prisoner-of-War. He was forced to take charge of a labor party and assigned the task of constructing slit trenches for bomb protection. Through self-effacing courage and sheer audacity of purpose, he caused to be constructed under the very eyes and alert surveillance of Japanese guards, a huge sign "U.S." This was done by rearranging the construction work of the slit trenches from the Japanese approved plan to one of his own devising, after causing the Japanese to concur in the changes suggested. The sign, if recognized by the Japanese, would have resulted in Antrim's immediate beheading, but Antrim's well-thought plan would result in Allied photographs indicating the occupants of the trenches and thus save hundreds of prisoners' lives.

The actions of Lieutenant Antrim that resulted in these two awards are admirable, but they are not unlike such similarly heroic actions of many other American soldiers, sailors, and marines. But one fateful day in April 1942, Richard Nott Antrim did something unbelievable. It was a deed that went beyond valor. It was a deed of rare nobility so profound that, as returning prisoners of war circulated the story, it captured the imagination and spoke volumes about selfless service and sacrifice. The award of the Medal of Honor by President Harry S. Truman on January 30, 1947, recognized the deed for its valor. As was his custom at these presentations, he told the naval hero, "I would rather have this medal than be president." Then the president did something unusual, recognizing Antrim's incredible actions for their nobility added this addendum: "You did a mighty fine thing!"

One hundred and fifty anxious faces looked back at the USS *Pope,* slowly sinking into a watery grave. The ship "that was old enough to vote," an old four-stack destroyer, had served well during its short combat career. The Battle of the Java Sea was its third major engagement. It was only three months after Pearl Harbor, and the Japanese ruled the Pacific. A massive force of enemy cruisers and destroyers sought to encircle Java, an island of the Malay Archipelago. As darkness fell on the eve of February 28, 1942, three ships slipped out of Surabaya in a desperate attempt to escape the snare the enemy was creating. Two of the ships were British, the heavy cruiser HMS *Exeter* and the destroyer HMS *Encounter*. The third was the USS *Pope*.

Through the night they had quietly tried to elude the enemy, but with daylight they were spotted by enemy aircraft and quickly engaged by nearby enemy cruisers and destroyers. All three ships fought valiantly, but in vain. The *Exeter* and *Encounter* quickly sank, and the badly damaged *Pope* was spared the same fate only by being hidden in a passing rain squall. The reprieve was only temporary. Damaged by enemy shells and bombs from Japanese carrier-launched aircraft, the *Pope* had slowly begun to sink.

As the sun set across the ocean, it would have been a night for panic and terror, were it not for the courage of the *Pope*'s executive officer, Lieutenant Richard Nott Antrim. As the ship had begun its slow descent to the ocean floor, he had organized life rafts and a single whaleboat to bear the 151-man crew to safety. Despite wounds from the earlier engagement, he struggled through the pain to lead and encourage his men. With great foresight he had attempted to insure provisions for an ordeal at sea, then distributed the meager rations among the men. All but one of the *Pope*'s crew survived the sinking, a tribute to Antrim's cool, effective leadership. But for them all, the greatest ordeal still lay ahead.

For three days the sailors remained together in a tight group, enduring the heat of the tropical sun, a merciless ocean, and a shortage of food and water. Richard Antrim's calm voice, effective leadership, and valiant example held them together. Then, on March 5, they were plucked from the sea—by a Japanese war ship. They became prisoners of war, taken to Makassar in the Celebes, one of the larger islands that was firmly under the control of the Japanese army. It was there that not only allegiances, but customs, collided.

Bushido is a Japanese word meaning "the way of the warrior." It was an ancient code with roots in feudal Japan, a code that demanded endurance, courage, and other warriorlike traits. It also demanded that any warrior who forfeited his honor in any way should take his own life rather than live in dishonor. To the Japanese soldiers of World War II, a prisoner was a warrior who had forfeited his honor and should have taken his own life. For this reason their hatred of Americans as enemies at war, turned to absolute disdain toward prisoners of war. Bushido justified, for the Japanese captor, subhuman treatment of prisoners, men the Japanese considered to be cowards and unworthy of respect. Torture was common, arbitrary, and deadly. This was the fate that awaited the crew of the *Pope* when they joined more than twenty-five hundred other prisoners at the POW camp at Makassar.

For weeks the prisoners had lived in fear, watched fellow prisoners broken and abused by sadistic guards who viewed their lives as something lower than the most basic animal life forms. Cries of pain and anguish filled the long nights, and the sights of death were seen with the dawn of each heart-rending day.

Hope quickly vanished as prisoners did their best to avoid eye contact with the enemy and struggled to obey each order to the ultimate degree. They had seen time and again how quickly, how cruelly, and how deadly the slightest infraction could be.

Time lost meaning. All that the prisoners could do was hope to survive each night, then pray for the end of each day. Tension mounted on both sides, and the situation was extremely volatile. It could erupt into mass murder at any moment for the slightest reason, or even for no reason at all. It was in this climate that the 2,700 prisoners watched in pained agony as one lieutenant failed to bow low enough to a Japanese guard one horrible day in April. As was expected—and all too common—the reaction was swift and violent.

The Japanese guard flew into a rage, venting all of his anger in a swift series of abusing blows from his swagger stick. It was an insane, violent flurry of blows that broke the skin and crushed the body of the lieutenant. Those Japanese guards who witnessed it felt no compassion, content to believe the battered lieutenant was receiving all he deserved and perhaps not enough. The frightened prisoners could not but look on helplessly, knowing that the slightest movement might draw attention to them and result in a similar or worse fate. But Lieutenant Richard Nott Antrim had had enough. His heart breaking for the lieutenant, he stepped forward—calling attention to himself to plead for mercy. It was an act that could have been perceived as insane as the wrath the guard vented on his victim, a hopeless gesture that could only result in two deaths instead of one. But it was an act the naval lieutenant believed had to be done, regardless of the cost.

With the broken body of one lieutenant lying at their feet, Lieutenant Antrim faced the enraged guard to plead the case of his brother. Struggling with broken Japanese and gestures, he tried to convince the guard that enough had been done, that the lieutenant had meant no insult. His sincere effort drew the attention of the entire force of enemy guards. Fellow prisoners looked on in amazement and fear, certain bad was about to turn worse. It also attracted the attention of the Japanese commander. Antrim continued to appeal the lieutenant's case, begging for mercy. In the center of the prison compound with trigger happy guards on one side and the abused and demoralized prison population on the other, a "kangaroo court" was held. There would be no mercy. Antrim was ordered to step back while the nearly unconscious lieutenant received his "just sentence"—fifty lashes with a thick, raw hawser.

The helpless lieutenant was already near death from his earlier beating as the first lash of the hawser landed across his body, only to be followed by another, and another, and another. Large welts broke open to spill his blood on the ground and, like a swarm of hungry sharks, the frenzy of the guard administering the punishment created a bloodlust. Fifteen lashes had left the man unconscious, unable to move or flinch from the repeated beating. Three more guards rushed into the scene, brutally kicking at the prostrate form. Further lashes would fall upon a body that could feel no more pain unless something happened.

It did!

"Enough!" spoke the voice of Lieutenant Richard Nott Antrim as a stunned silence fell over the camp at his unprecedented action.

"I'll take the rest!" Lieutenant Antrim said.

Prisoners could only stare in incredulity. The Japanese were stunned. They had never expected to see such an act of unselfish, personal sacrifice by any of the prisoners they despised as subhuman. So stunning was the proclamation, no one on either side of the camp could believe what their ears had heard. Lieutenant Antrim had to repeat his offer.

"If there is to be fifty lashes, I will take the rest of them for him."

This time his stunning pronouncement sunk in. From the ranks of the battered, broken prisoners there erupted a roar of acclaim. Among the Japanese guards there was nothing but silence, amazement, and a slow dawning of what had just occurred. It was a defining moment, one of those rare experiences that is so magnificent and powerful, none can deny it. The punishment ended, and a young naval officer's broken body gradually healed because Richard Nott Antrim cared enough to show the highest degree of brotherhood—unconditional love.

In the years that followed, torture and abuse continued. But the actions of Lieutenant Antrim that day in April gave the Japanese guards a new appreciation for their prisoners, and the torture and beatings lessened for a time. For the hopeless men who struggled to find reason to continue, to survive in the living hell to which they had been cast, there was a new inspiration.

On January 17, 1943, station J.L.G.4, Tokyo, broadcast a message, read by a Japanese announcer and written by Richard Nott Antrim. It read: "Dear Mother: The Japanese have given me permission to send a message and I am sending you my love. I am treated fine and in good health. I want you to write in care of the War Prisoners' Information Bureau in Tokyo, through the International Red Cross at Geneva, Switzerland. Love, Dick."

Two and a half more years remained before he would see his family again. When he was liberated in September 1945, he returned home to continue his service in the United States Navy. He never sought recognition, only to serve others. His valor on a momentous day in April 1942 became known only because it was an act other returning POWs couldn't help telling the story to others. On January 30, 1947, President Truman invited Commander Antrim to the White House to award him the Medal of Honor with that simple understatement, "You did a mighty fine thing."

On a chilly April day in 1969, the sound of "Taps" echoed across the hillsides where warriors rest in Arlington National Cemetery. Beneath a flag-draped casket rested the body of a hero that far too few people ever met. Most of his neighbors back home in Arkansas saw Dick Antrim in uniform for the first time as the newspapers announced the death of a humble, quiet man whose first concern had always been for other people.[1]

Admiral Antrim's story speaks to his courage and to the sacrifice he was willing to make for a fellow prisoner.

In his offer to share the other's beating, we are reminded of the gashes on the back of our Savior who suffered for us. "Surely he hath borne our griefs, and carried our sorrows: yet we did esteem him stricken, smitten of God, and afflicted. But he was wounded for our transgressions; he was bruised for our iniquities: the chastisement of our peace was upon him; and with his stripes we are healed" (Isaiah 53:4, 5, KJV).

The Gift of a Meal

O NE OF MY MOST MEMORABLE COMMUNIONS WAS THE TIME WE SHOWED THE *classic film* Babette's Feast *as we ate the bread and drank the juice. In that festive ceremony, we were reminded of our shared covenant to bond as a community over this sacred meal and in one voice, "proclaim the Lord's death until he comes" (1 Corinthians 11:26).*

∾

Isak Dinesen tells a delightful story about an austere, fundamentalist community in Denmark. A young woman named Babette worked as a cook for two elderly sisters who were not aware that Babette formerly was a skilled chef for nobility in her native France. Babette dreamed of returning to her beloved city of Paris. So every year she had a friend in Paris purchase a lottery ticket for her, banking on the slim chance she could score enough cash to return to Paris.

Every evening her frugal employers insisted that she prepare the same ho-hum meal: boiled fish and potatoes. After all, they reasoned, Jesus taught, "Take no thought of food and drink" (see Matthew 6:25, 31).

Then the improbable happened! Babette won the lottery of ten thousand francs—no small fortune. To the villagers' surprise, Babette insisted on creating an authentic French dining experience for them.

"Absolutely not," the townspeople protested. "It would be a sin to indulge in such rich food."

"Please," Babette begged. "After all, this could be my only chance to do what I've always wanted to do."

At last the townspeople consented. "As a favor to you, we will allow you to serve us this French dinner." Privately, the people vowed not to enjoy the banquet. Instead of savoring Babette's delicacies, they determined to occupy their minds on spiritual matters such as fasting and prayer. They reasoned that God would forgive their indulgence if they did not enjoy it.

Babette threw herself into the preparation with reckless abandon. Loads of exotic food arrived in the village. Meats, cheeses, spices, and exotic fruits and vegetables—no expense was spared in securing the finest fare.

At last the banquet was ready to be served and the village gathered. The first course was a scrumptious turtle soup. The diners politely ate it, but without enjoyment. Although it was their tradition to eat in silence, on this evening they permitted conversation. With the appetizers, the atmosphere brightened. Someone smiled. Another giggled. Still another draped his arm over a friend's shoulder. "Hey!" he explained, "The Lord Jesus did say, 'Love one another.' " By the time the quail entrée arrived, those stern, pleasure-paranoid people were chuckling and slurping and guffawing and singing praises to God for their many years together.

One meal and the pious pessimists were transformed into a loving community. One of the two sisters followed Babette into the kitchen, bubbling, "Oh, how we will miss you when you return to Paris!"

Babette replied, "I will not be returning to Paris, because I have no money. I spent it all on the feast."

The story brings to mind Someone else who gave His all to make us a loving community through the gift of a meal. "Whenever you share in this meal," Jesus explained, "you celebrate My sacrifice for you."

This is Communion. The body of Christ celebrates His broken body. The community rejoices in His spilled blood. The church determines to proclaim the good news of the new covenant.

Sara Miles remembers fondly her first experience with Communion. It changed her life forever. She writes the following:

> One early, cloudy morning, when I was forty-six, I walked into a church, ate a piece of bread, took a sip of wine. A routine Sunday activity for tens of millions of Americans—except that up until that moment I'd led a thoroughly secular life, at best indifferent to religion, more often appalled by its fundamentalist crusades. This was my first communion. It changed everything. . . .
>
> . . . The mysterious sacrament turned out to be not a symbolic wafer at all but actual food—indeed, the bread of life. In that shocking moment of communion, filled with a deep desire to reach for and become part of a body, I realized that what I'd been doing with my life all along was what I was meant to do: feed people.
>
> And so I did. I took communion, I passed the bread to others, and then I kept going, compelled to find new ways to share what I had experienced. I started a food pantry and gave away literally tons of fruit and vegetables and cereal around the same altar where I'd first received the body of Christ. I organized new pantries all over my city to provide hundreds and hundreds of hungry families with free groceries each week.[1]

If Communion does not spill outside the walls of the church, then it fails in its God-ordained purpose. "Whenever you eat this bread and drink this cup," Jesus instructed, we are to "proclaim the Lord's death" (1 Corinthians 11:26). We are to share the good news of forgiveness and reconciliation, inviting everyone into the saving embrace of our loving Father.

Ellen White explains that when we come to the Communion table and behold our Savior's matchless love, we will "be elevated in thought, purified in heart, transformed in character. [We] will go forth to be a light to the world, to reflect in some degree this mysterious love."[2]

So now, go—and reflect this mysterious love.

⁓⋄

Jesus Dies on the Cross

By Jerry D. Thomas

C HAPTER 78, "CALVARY," FROM THE DESIRE OF AGES HAS BEEN MOST HELP-
ful in my study of God's sacrifice—His spilled blood and broken body. I especially appreciate the book Messiah, a contemporary adaptation by Jerry D.
Thomas of the classic book. This chapter is reprinted, with my heartfelt gratitude, from
Thomas's paraphrase.

～

The news that Jesus had been condemned to die spread quickly, and people
of all types flocked toward the place of crucifixion. The priests had agreed not
to harass Jesus' disciples when Judas agreed to betray Him, so many disciples and
followers of Jesus joined the crowds.

Three crosses had been prepared for Barabbas and two of his thieves who
were scheduled to die that day. The cross that had been ready for Barabbas was
placed on Jesus' bleeding shoulders. Since the Passover supper, Jesus had had
nothing to eat or drink. He had suffered the pain of being betrayed and abandoned. He had been rushed from Annas to Caiaphas to Pilate to Herod and
back to Pilate. The night had been filled with events that would test the heart
of any human. Jesus hadn't failed. He had taken it all with dignity. But after the
second beating with the whip, when the cross was laid on His shoulder, His human body could take no more. Jesus collapsed.

The crowd showed no mercy, taunting Jesus because He couldn't carry the
cross. The soldiers lifted the cross up and placed it on Him again. Again Jesus fell
to the ground. When it was clear that Jesus could not carry the cross, they began
to search for someone who could. No Jew would carry it because this would
make him unclean for Passover.

Then Simon, a stranger from Cyrene, met the crowd as he came into the city.
Simon, astonished at what he saw, expressed pity for the poor Man. So the soldiers
seized him and forced him to carry the cross for Jesus. Simon's sons were followers
of Jesus, but Simon was not. Carrying the cross to Calvary turned out to be a real
blessing for Simon, because he became a believer in the Messiah that day.

Many women were in the crowd that followed the Savior. Some had brought their sick loved ones to Him to be healed—others had been healed themselves. They were shocked at how the crowd hated Jesus. When Jesus fell under the cross, these women ignored the angry priests and began wailing with sorrow.

Even in His pain and exhaustion, Jesus noticed. He knew that they didn't understand who He was or His sacrifice for them, but He appreciated their sympathy. He said, " 'Women of Jerusalem, don't cry for me. Cry for yourselves and for your children' " (Luke 23:28).[1]

He looked ahead to the time when Jerusalem would be destroyed, and some of these same women would die along with their children.

In the destruction of Jerusalem, Jesus saw a symbol of the end of the world. He said, " 'Then people will say to the mountains, "Fall on us!" And they will say to the hills, "Cover us!" If they act like this now when life is good, what will happen when bad times come?' " (Luke 23:30, 31). God's anger against sin was now focused on His Son. What would the suffering be like at the end for someone who refused to give up sin?

In the crowd that followed Jesus to Calvary were many who had shouted the hosannas and waved palm branches when He rode into Jerusalem. More than a few who had shouted praises that day with everyone else, now joined in screaming, "Crucify him!" When Jesus rode into Jerusalem, His disciples pressed close around Him and felt the honor. Now they followed Him at a distance to escape the humiliation.

Jesus' mother

When they reached the place of execution, the two thieves fought those who forced them onto their crosses. Jesus did not resist. Mary, His mother, supported by John, had followed her Son's steps to Calvary. She wanted so much to put her hand under His head and comfort Him, but this was not permitted. She still held on to the hope that Jesus would save Himself. But in her heart she remembered that He had predicted these events.

As the thieves were bound to their crosses, Mary held her breath. Would the One who could bring the dead to life allow Himself to be crucified? Must she give up her faith that He was the Messiah? She saw His hands stretched out on the rough wood and the hammer raised up. When the spikes were driven through His tender flesh, Mary fainted. The disciples carried her away.

The Savior is sacrificed

Jesus did not cry out, but great drops of sweat formed on His forehead. No caring hands wiped His face, no words of comfort or sympathy were spoken to sooth His human heart. While the soldiers went about their dreadful work, Jesus prayed, "Father, forgive them, because they don't know what they are doing."

Jesus didn't call down curses on these soldiers who handled Him so roughly.

He didn't call for revenge on the priests and leaders. He only breathed a prayer for their forgiveness because they didn't understand what they were doing. But this ignorance didn't take away their guilt. They could have learned about Jesus and accepted Him as their Savior. Some of them would see their sins, repent, and change. Others, by not repenting, would make it impossible for Jesus' prayer to be answered. But God's plan was being completed—Jesus was earning the right to represent all humans to His Father.

Jesus' prayer for His enemies included every sinner from the beginning of the world to the end of time. All of us are guilty of crucifying the Son of God. But all are offered forgiveness.

As soon as Jesus was nailed to the cross, it was lifted up by strong men and shoved into its hole in the rock—causing intense pain for Jesus. Then Pilate had a board inscribed with the words "Jesus of Nazareth, King of the Jews" nailed to the cross above Jesus' head.

This irritated the Jews. But they had claimed Caesar as their true king. The sign declared that whoever else claimed to be king in Israel would be killed. In order to have Jesus killed, the priests had sacrificed their national identity. But they asked Pilate to change the words to "This man said, 'I am the King of the Jews.'"

Pilate, already angry with himself, replied coldly, "What I have written, I have written."

God guided the hand that wrote the inscription. People from many lands were in Jerusalem, and that sign declaring that Jesus was the Messiah was noticed. Many people went back to the Scriptures to study the prophecies.

Many prophecies were fulfilled as Jesus suffered on the cross. From the Psalms came predictions that the Messiah's hands and feet would be pierced, and that others would gamble for His clothes. The soldiers at the Crucifixion were given the prisoners' clothes to destroy or keep. Since Jesus' coat was one seamless piece of woven cloth, the soldiers gambled to decide which of them would keep it.

Another prediction from Psalms said that the suffering Messiah would be offered vinegar to drink. Those who suffered death on the cross were allowed to have a drink that would dull their pain. But when Jesus tasted it, He refused to drink it. He needed a clear mind to keep focused on God, His only strength. Clouding His senses would only give Satan an advantage.

The Jewish priests and leaders joined the mob in mocking the dying Savior. "If you are the Son of God, come down from there," they shouted. "If he is the Messiah, let him save himself." Satan and his angels—in human form—were there encouraging the priests and stirring up the mob.

The Father's voice from heaven was silent, and no one else spoke up for Jesus. He suffered alone. He heard the priests declare, "If he really is the Messiah, let him come down from the cross. Then we will believe in him." Jesus could have come down from the cross. But because He didn't save Himself, sinners have the hope of forgiveness.

One thief believes

Jesus felt one gleam of comfort on the cross—the prayer of the repentant thief. Both of the men crucified with Jesus had mocked Him at first, and one only became more desperate and defiant as he suffered. But the other was not a hardened criminal. He was less guilty than many who stood beside the cross cursing the Savior. He had seen Jesus and heard Him teach, but had been convinced by the priests not to listen. Trying to quiet his conscience, he plunged into a criminal life until he was arrested and condemned.

On the cross he saw the religious teachers ridicule Jesus. He heard his fellow thief shout, "If you are the Messiah, save yourself and us." Among the crowd he heard many telling stories of what Jesus had done and said. Once again, he felt sure that this was the Messiah. He turned to the other thief and said, "You should fear God! You are getting the same punishment He is." The thieves were beyond fearing humans, but one of them realized that there was a God to fear. To the other thief he said, "We are getting what we deserve, but this Man has done nothing wrong."

When he was condemned for his crime, the thief had given up all hope. But now strange, gentle thoughts were stirring in his mind. The Holy Spirit led his thinking step by step until it all made sense to him. In spite of being mocked and hanging on a cross, he saw Jesus as the Lamb of God. Hope mingled with the pain in his voice as he said, "Lord, remember me when You come into Your kingdom."

Quickly the answer came in a voice full of love and power: "Today I tell you the truth—you will be with Me in paradise."

Jesus had listened with a longing heart for some words of faith from His disciples. Instead He had only heard sad doubts: "We believed that He was the One who would save Israel." The dying thief's words of faith encouraged Jesus when no one else would even acknowledge Him.

Those words of faith also got the attention of bystanders. The soldiers gambling over Jesus' clothes stopped to listen. As Jesus spoke His promise, a ray of living light pierced the dark cloud that seemed to cover the cross. Jesus, hanging there in shame, was bathed in glory. Heaven recognized Him as the Bearer of sin. Humans could strip Him of His clothing, but they could not take His power to forgive sins and save all who came to God through Him.

Jesus did not promise that the thief would be with Him in paradise that same day. He Himself did not go to heaven that day. On the morning of the Resurrection, He said, "I have not yet gone up to My Father." But the promise was given "today"—right then as He hung dying on the cross—and the forgiven thief will be with Jesus in heaven.

Jesus was placed in the middle between the two thieves at the request of the priests to show that He was the worst of the criminals. But in the same way, His cross was placed in the middle of a dying world trapped in sin. And His words of forgiveness to the thief are a light that shines hope to the farthest parts of the world. During His suffering, Jesus spoke as a prophet to the women of Jerusalem. As a priest or representative, He asked His Father to forgive His murderers. As the Savior, He forgave the sins of a repented thief.

Mary, His mother, returned to the foot of the cross, supported by John. She couldn't bear to be away from her Son, and John, knowing that the end was near, brought her back. Looking into her grief-filled eyes, Jesus said, "Dear woman, here is your son." Then He said to John, "Here is your mother."

John understood and accepted the responsibility. From that moment he cared for Mary in his own home. Jesus had no money to leave for His mother's care, but He gave her what she needed most—a friend who loved her because she loved Jesus. John was greatly blessed as well—she was a constant reminder of his beloved Master. Those who follow Jesus will never leave their parents without care or respect.

The death of Jesus

Now the Lord of glory was near death, feeling agony in both body and soul. It wasn't the fear of death or the pain of the cross that caused His suffering. It was a sense of the horrible wickedness of sin. Jesus saw how few humans would be willing to break their addiction to it. Without help from God, all humans would be exterminated.

The guilt of every human since Adam was placed on Jesus—our Substitute—and it pressed heavily on His heart. All of His life, Jesus had been sharing the good news of the Father's forgiving love. But now with this terrible weight of sin on Him, He could not see the Father's face. This tore at His heart in a way that humans will never fully understand. This agony was so overwhelming that He hardly felt the physical pain.

Satan pressed Jesus' heart with fierce temptations. He did not feel the hope that He would rise from the grave or that the Father would accept His sacrifice. Jesus felt the anguish a sinner will feel when no One pleads for mercy for the guilty. It was this sense of sin—the sense that the Father's anger was focused on Him as the One taking the place of sinful humans—that broke His heart.

The sun refused to look down on this awful scene. Its bright rays had been lighting the earth at noon when suddenly it seemed to be blotted out. The whole land was dark until three o'clock in the afternoon. This unnatural darkness was as deep as midnight without moon or stars. It was a miraculous sign given by God to strengthen our faith.

God and the holy angels were there beside the cross, hidden in the thick darkness. The Father was with His Son. But His presence had to be hidden. In that terrible hour, Jesus could not be comforted by His Father's presence.

God created the darkness to cover the last human suffering of His Son. All who had seen Jesus suffer that day had been convicted of His divinity. His long hours of torture had been accompanied by the stares and jeers of the mob. Now, mercifully, God hid Him.

When the darkness came, an unexplainable terror came over the crowd gathered around the cross. The cursing and shouting stopped. Brilliant lightning occasionally flashed through the clouds and revealed the crucified Savior. Priests, leaders, soldiers, and the mob thought their payback was coming. Some whispered that Jesus would now come down from the cross.

At three o'clock the darkness lifted from the crowd but still covered Jesus. No one could see through the gloom that shrouded His suffering soul. But Jesus' voice was heard crying, " 'My God, my God, why have you rejected me?' " (Matthew 27:46).

Many voices suggested that Jesus was being punished for claiming to be God. Many of His followers who heard His despairing cry gave up all hope. If God had rejected Jesus, what could His followers trust?

Then the darkness lifted and Jesus revived enough to feel the physical pain. He said, "I am thirsty." One of the Roman soldiers felt pity and offered Jesus a sponge soaked in vinegar. But the priests mocked Jesus again. They misinterpreted Jesus' cry to mean that He was calling for the prophet Elijah. They refused to relieve His thirst. "No," they said, "we want to see if Elijah will come and save him."

He did it for you

The perfect Son of God hung on the cross, His skin slashed by whips. His hands that had so often reached out to bless others were nailed to the wooden boards. His feet, so tireless on missions of love, were spiked to the beam. His royal head was pierced by the crown of thorns; His trembling lips twisted in a cry of pain.

And all that He suffered—the blood that dripped from His head, His hands, and His feet, the agony that tore His body with every breath, and the unspeakable anguish in His heart from being separated from His Father—speaks to each of us, saying, "For you the Son of God agrees to carry this guilt; for you He battles death and wins; for you He opens the gates of heaven; for you He offers Himself as a sacrifice. All of this He does because of His love for you."

Jesus dies triumphantly

Suddenly the darkness lifted from the cross. In a voice that seemed to ring through all creation like a trumpet, Jesus cried, "It is finished. Father, I give You My life." A light surrounded the cross, and the Savior's face shone like the glory of the sun. Then He hung His head and died.

In the darkness, Jesus drank the cup of human suffering and sin. During those dreadful hours, He was sustained by what He had known all His life. By faith, He rested in His Father's love even though He could no longer feel it. As

He surrendered His life to God, the sense of having lost His Father's love vanished. By faith, Jesus won the battle.

Now darkness covered the land again, and there was a violent earthquake. In the surrounding mountains, rocks split into pieces and crashed to the plains below. Graves were ripped open and the dead were thrown out. Priests, soldiers, and the others in the crowd fell to the ground in fear.

The moment Jesus cried, "It is finished," was the time of the evening sacrifice at the temple. The lamb that represented the Messiah had been brought in to be killed. The priest stood with the knife in his hand as the people watched. Then the ground trembled, because the Lord Himself was approaching. With a loud ripping sound, the inner curtain of the temple was torn from top to bottom. People stared right into the place that was once filled with the presence of God. The Most Holy Place of the temple was no longer sacred.

There was terror and confusion everywhere. The knife fell from the priest's suddenly numb hand and the lamb escaped. The symbolic intersected with reality. The great sacrifice had been made. A new, living path to salvation was available to everyone. Jesus would now become our Priest, our Representative in heaven.[2]

Endnotes

Preface
1. Ellen G. White, *Testimonies for the Church* (Mountain View, Calif.: Pacific Press® Publishing Association, 1948), 4:374.
2. Marcus Luttrell, *Lone Survivor* (New York: Little, Brown and Company, 2007), 238.
3. Ibid.
4. Ellen G. White, *The Great Controversy* (Mountain View, Calif.: Pacific Press®, 1950), 651.
5. First Corinthians 11:24. Unless otherwise noted, all Scripture references are from the New International Version.

Chapter 1
1. This story is shared in memory of its author, Robert Surridge. Originally published in C. Blake and L. Peckham, eds., *"Insight" Presents More Unforgettable Stories* (Hagerstown, Md.: Review and Herald® Publishing Association, 1996), 180–183. Reprinted by permission of the author's wife, Dawn Noorbergen Surridge.

Chapter 2
1. *Wikipedia* contributors, "Scio, New York," *Wikipedia,* accessed February 24, 2012, http://en.wikipedia.org/wiki/Scio,_New_York.
2. Anthony Violanti, "War's Sacrifice," *Buffalo News,* June 30, 2005, accessed November 16, 2011, http://www.rusoffagency.com/authors/phillips_m/thegift_ofvalor/thegift_ofvalor_buffalonews_feature.htm.
3. "Jason Dunham to Enter Section V Basketball Hall of Fame," *Wellsville Daily Reporter,* July 9, 2010, accessed February 24, 2012, http://www.wellsvilledaily.com/features/x1876488637/Jason-Dunham-to-enter-Section-V-Basketball-Hall-of-Fame.
4. Violanti, "War's Sacrifice."
5. Michael M. Phillips, *The Gift of Valor: A War Story* (New York: Broadway Books, 2005), 15.
6. Michael M. Phillips, "In Combat, Marine Put Theory to Test, Comrades Believe Cpl. Dunham's Quick Action in Face of a Grenade Saved 2 Lives, They Say 'No, No—Watch His Hand!' " *Wall Street Journal,* May 25, 2004, A1, accessed February 24, 2012, http://online.wsj.com/article/0,,SB108543666009520024,00.html.
7. Ibid.
8. David Sharp, "Warship Honors Marine Who Died Protecting Comrades," *Seattle Times,* July 30, 2009, accessed February 24, 2012, http://seattletimes.nwsource.com/html/nationworld/2009570840_apusherowarshipchristening.html.
9. Michael M. Phillips, "Marine Put Theory to Test."
10. Ibid.
11. Ibid.
12. Catharine Young, "Amity Bridge & Highway to Be Renamed After Scio Hero Jason Dunham," New York Senate, August 5, 2011, accessed November 22, 2011, http://www.nysenate.gov/press-release/amity-bridge-highway-be-renamed-after-scio-hero-jason-dunham-1.

13. Paul A. Jannace, "Dunham Receives the Ultimate Honor for the Ultimate Sacrifice," Jason's Memorial, accessed November 22, 2011, http://www.jasonsmemorial.org/art_wellesville.pdf.

14. *Wikipedia* contributors, "Jason Dunham," *Wikipedia,* accessed June 21, 2012, http://en.wikipedia.org/wiki/Jason_Dunham.

15. Gina Cavallaro, "Cpl. Jason Dunham: Marine, Hero, Destroyer," *Marine Corps Times,* November 12, 2010, accessed February 24, 2012, http://militarytimes.com/blogs/battle-rattle/2010/11/12/cpl-jason-dunham-marine-hero-destroyer/.

16. Dai Hankey, "Lessons I've Learned From My Little Girl—4. Baby Jesus," *Sanctified Rant* (blog), May 26, 2009, accessed February 24, 2012, https://sanctifiedrant.wordpress.com/2009/05/26/lessons-ive-learned-from-my-little-girl-4-baby-jesus/.

Chapter 3
1. "Greater Love," by Violet L. M. Curtis. Originally published in *The Youth's Instructor,* September 15, 1942, 5, 13, accessed February 20, 2012, http://www.adventistarchives.org/docs/YI/YI19420915-V90-37__C.pdf. Reprinted by permission of the author.

Chapter 4
1. Father Edward Schmidt, SJ, "One Faith, and the Many Forms of Violence," *Company Magazine,* accessed August 26, 2010, http://www.companymagazine.org/v154/onefaith.html. Reprinted by permission of the author.

Chapter 5
1. Floyd Miller, "Ned's Legacy," *Reader's Digest,* January 1971, 42, 43.

2. Caroline Richmond, "Herbert Scheinberg: Physician and Expert on Hereditary Diseases," Obituary, June 21, 2009, accessed February 25, 2012, http://www.guardian.co.uk/science/2009/jun/22/herbert-scheinberg-obituary-wilsons-disease.

3. Miller, "Ned's Legacy," 46.

4. Ellen G. White, *Sermons and Talks* (Silver Spring, Md.: Ellen G. White Estate, 1994), 2:169.

5. Bart Gavigan, Jim Hanon, and Bill Ewing, *End of the Spear,* directed by Jim Hanon (Oklahoma City, Okla.: EthnoGraphic Media, 2006).

Chapter 6
1. "A Change of Heart," *Dateline NBC,* airing on October 1, 1999.

2. "Miles" by Nichole Nordeman, Copyright © 2005 Birdwing Music (ASCAP) Birdboy Songs (ASCAP) (admin. at EMICMGPublishing.com). All rights reserved. Used by permission of Birdwing Music.

3. Kelly St. James, "Grieving Mom Comforted as Part of Her Son Lives On," *San Francisco Chronicle,* September 11, 2004, accessed June 27, 2012, http://www.sfgate.com/bayarea/article/SAN-FRANCISCO-Grieving-mom-comforted-as-part-of-2694743.php. Used by permission of the *San Francisco Chronicle.*

Chapter 7
1. Max Lucado, "A Satisfied Thirst," in *The Applause of Heaven* (Nashville, Tenn.: Thomas Nelson, Inc., 1990), 91–93. Reprinted by permission. All rights reserved.

Chaper 8
1. Kate Benson, "Transplant Girl's Blood Change a 'Miracle,'" *Sydney Morning Herald,* January 25, 2008, accessed February 25, 2012, http://www.smh.com.au/news/national/transplant-girl-a-miracle/2008/01/24/1201157559928.html.

2. Zandolie, January 24, 2008 (12:23 P.M.), comment on Truetrini SC, "Wow, Unheard of and Almost Unbelievable!" Soca Warriors Online Forum, January 24, 2008, accessed February 25, 2012, http://www.socawarriors.net/forum/index.php?PHPSESSID=701cb02692115c0e6e31ebe0901dbbeb&topic=33431.msg388417#msg388417.

3. Truetrini SC, "Wow, Unheard of and Almost Unbelievable!"

4. Benson, "Transplant Girl's Blood Change a 'Miracle.'"

5.   Ibid.

6.   Einat Rotman, "The Miracle of Spontaneous Blood-Type Switch," *Future of Things,* February 4, 2008, accessed February 25, 2012, http://thefutureofthings.com/news/1104/the-miracle-of -spontaneous-blood-type-switch.html.

7.   Michael Stormon, "Liver Transplant Patient Hailed a 'Medical Miracle,' " January 24, 2008, transcript, Australian Broadcasting Corporation Radio, http://www.abc.net.au/pm/content/2007 /s2146056.htm.

8.   Kate Benson, " 'Too Strange to Be True': Mum's Little Hero Takes on Blood Type of Liver Donor," *Age,* January 25, 2008, accessed February 25, 2012, http://www.theage.com .au/news/national/too-strange-to-be-true-mums-little-hero-takes-on-blood-type-ofliver -donor/2008/01/24/1201157560407.html.

9.   Ibid.

10.   Rotman, "The Miracle of Spontaneous Blood-Type Switch."

11.   Sean Rubinsztein-Dunlop, "Aust Doctors Hail Teen's Transplant 'Miracle,' " *ABC News,* January 28, 2008, accessed December 12, 2011, http://www.abc.net.au/news/2008-01-24 /aust-doctors-hail-teens-transplant-miracle/1023688.

12.   Benson, "Transplant Girl's Blood Change a 'Miracle.' "

Chaper 9

1.   Carl P. Cosaert, "My Journey With Jairus," *Adventist Review,* November 23, 2006, accessed February 20, 2012, http://www.adventistreview.org/article/845/archives/issue-2006-1533 /my-journey-with-jairus. Reprinted by permission of the author.

2.   Mark Witas, *Live Out Loud* (Hagerstown, Md.: Review and Herald®, 2011), 65–68. Reprinted by permission of the author.

Chapter 10

1.   Wikipedia contributors, "2008 Mumbai Attacks," *Wikipedia,* accessed February 25, 2012, http://en.wikipedia.org/wiki/2008_Mumbai_attacks.

2.   Mark Magnier and Subhash Sharma, "Terror Attacks Ravage Mumbai," *Los Angeles Times,* November 27, 2008, accessed December 16, 2011, http://articles.latimes.com/print/2008/nov/27 /world/fg-mumbai27.

3.   Marie Brenner, "Anatomy of a Siege," *Vanity Fair,* November 2009, accessed December 12, 2011, http://www.vanityfair.com/politics/features/2009/11/taj-hotel-siege-200911.

4.   Ravi Zacharias, *Has Christianity Failed You?* (Grand Rapids, Mich.: Zondervan, 2010), 42.

5.   Ibid.

6.   Ellen G. White, *Testimonies to Ministers and Gospel Workers* (Mountain View, Calif.: Pacific Press®, 1962), 517.

Chapter 11

1.   Helen Rezatto, "Girl Against a Blizzard," *Reader's Digest,* March 1962, 83–87. Reprinted with permission from *Reader's Digest.* Copyright © 1962 by The Reader's Digest Association, Inc.

Chapter 13

1.   *Wikipedia* contributors, "Arland D. Williams Jr.," *Wikipedia,* accessed August 8, 2012, http://en.wikipedia.org/w/index.php?title=Arland_D._Williams,_Jr.&oldid=500847362 quoted in "Arland D. Williams Jr.," Facebook, accessed February 17, 2012, http://www.facebook .com/pages/Arland-D-Williams-Jr/116504791731176?sk=info.

2.   Transcript of Air Florida Flight 90 cockpit voice recorder, "Air Florida Flight 90," *Wikipedia,* accessed August 8, 2012, http://en.wikipedia.org/wiki/Air_Florida_Flight_90.

3.   *Wikipedia* contributors, "Air Florida Flight 90," *Wikipedia,* accessed February 17, 2012, http://en.wikipedia.org/wiki/Air_Florida_Flight_90.

4.   Earl Babbie, *You Can Make a Difference,* accessed February 17, 2012, http://www1 .chapman.edu/~babbie/YCMAD/Ch02.html.

5.   "Arland D. Williams Jr.," Facebook.

6.   *Wikipedia* contributors, "Kelly Duncan," *Wikipedia,* accessed February 18, 2012,

http://en.wikipedia.org/wiki/Kelly_Duncan.

7. Wes Junker, quoted in Kevin Ambrose, "The 30 Year Anniversary of the Crash of Air Florida Flight 90," *Washington Post,* January 12, 2012, accessed February 17, 2012, http://www.washingtonpost.com/blogs/capital-weather-gang/post/the-30-year-anniversary-of-the-crash-of-air-florida-flight-90/2012/01/11/gIQAEVH4tP_blog.html.

8. Paul White, "Under the Curse," *Abundant Grace Daily Devotional* (blog), July 19, 2011, accessed February 18, 2012, http://paulwhiteministries.wordpress.com/tag/galatians/.

Chapter 14

1. *Wikipedia* contributors, "Auschwitz Concentration Camp," *Wikipedia,* accessed February 26, 2012, http://en.wikipedia.org/wiki/Auschwitz_concentration_camp.

2. Pope Paul VI, quoted in "Pope Honors Martyr," *Spokesman Review,* October 18, 1971, accessed February 26, 2012, http://news.google.com/newspapers?nid=1314&dat=19711018&id=3_tLAAAAIBAJ&sjid=juwDAAAAIBAJ&pg=7519,1292933.

3. " 'Greater Love Hath No Man—,' " *Adventist Review,* March 31, 1983, 17.

4. Louis Bülow, "Kolbe, the Saint From Auschwitz," *The Holocaust,* accessed August 26, 2010, http://www.auschwitz.dk/kolbe.htm.

5. Lawrence Elliott, "The Heroism of Father Kolbe," *Reader's Digest,* July 1973, 99.

6. Ibid., 97.

7. Ibid., 98.

8. Ibid.

9. Louis Bülow, "Father Kolbe," *Father Kolbe,* accessed February 26, 2012, http://www.fatherkolbe.com/content4.html.

10. Elliott, "The Heroism of Father Kolbe."

11. Bülow, "Kolbe, the Saint From Auschwitz."

12. Antonio Ricciardi, *St. Maximilian Kolbe: Apostle of Our Difficult Age* (Boston: Daughters of St. Paul, 1982), 308, 309.

Chapter 15

1. Jonathan Pearlman, "Jordan Tyson's Father Tells of His Death in Brisbane Floods," *Telegraph,* January 15, 2011, accessed January 16, 2011, http://www.telegraph.co.uk/news/worldnews/australiaandthepacific/australia/8262068/Jordan-Tysons-father-tells-of-his-death-in-Brisbane-floods.html.

2. Reuters, "Worst Disaster on Record for Queensland," *Stuff,* January 12, 2011, accessed February 26, 2012, http://www.stuff.co.nz/world/australia/4531356/Queenslanders-readied-for-more-tragedy.

3. Associated Press, "Woman Swept Away Drowns in Australian Floodwaters," *Seattle Times,* January 1, 2011, accessed August 9, 2012, http://seattletimes.nwsource.com/html/nationworld/2013818877_apasaustraliaflooding.html.

4. Richard Shears, "He'd Do Anything for Us, Says Family of Shy Boy Who Gave up His Life to Save His Brother From Raging Brisbane Floods," *Daily Mail,* January 14, 2011, accessed January 16, 2011, http://www.dailymail.co.uk/news/article-1346975/Hed-says-family-Jordan-Rice-gave-life-save-brother-raging-Brisbane-floods.html#ixzz1BG55NvER.

5. Amanda Gearing and Natasha Bita, "Take My Brother First: Heroic Final Acts Saves Sibling," *Australian,* January 13, 2011, accessed August 9, 2012, http://www.theaustralian.com.au/in-depth/queensland-floods/take-my-brother-first-heroic-final-act-saves-sibling/story-fn7iwx3v-1225986648911.

6. Greig Box-Turnbull, "Australia Floods: Dad Pays Tribute to Jordan Rice, the Teen Who Gave His Life for His Brother," *Daily Mirror,* January 17, 2011, accessed January 17, 2011, http://www.mirror.co.uk/news/top-stories/2011/01/17/australia-floods-dad-pays-tribute-to-jordan-rice-the-teen-who-gave-his-life-for-his-brother-115875-22854621/.

7. Sam Jones, "Australia Floods: 'The House Has Gone, The Car's Gone—Everything Apart From the Clothes We Had on Our Backs,' " *Guardian,* January 12, 2011, accessed August 9, 2012, http://www.guardian.co.uk/world/2011/jan/12/australia-floods-jordan-rice.

8. Shears, "He'd Do Anything for Us."
9. Box-Turnbull, "Australia Floods: Dad Pays Tribute to Jordan Rice."
10. Ibid.
11. Pearlman, "Jordan Tyson's Father Tells of His Death."

Chapter 16
1. Laurens van der Post, *The Seed and the Sower* (New York: William Morrow and Co., 1963), 50.
2. Ibid., 55, 56.
3. Ibid., 63, 64.
4. Ibid., 79.
5. Ibid., 80.
6. Ibid., 91.
7. Ibid., 92.
8. Ibid., 122.

Chapter 17
1. "To Forgive Is to Set a Prisoner Free," *Positive Quote of the Week* (blog), April 17, 2006, accessed February 27, 2012, http://positive-thought-of-the-week.blogspot.com/2006/04/to-forgive-is-to-set-prisoner-free.html.
2. Lewis B. Smedes, "Forgiveness—The Power to Change the Past," *Christianity Today*, January 7, 1983, accessed August 9, 2012, http://www.christianitytoday.com/ct/2002/decemberweb-only/12-16-55.0.html?start=2.
3. Ellen G. White, *Steps to Christ* (Mountain View, Calif.: Pacific Press®, 1956), 73.

Chapter 18
1 Julia C. Mead, "Deal in Turkey-Throwing Case After Victim Calls for Leniency," *New York Times*, August 16, 2005, accessed February 15, 2012, http://www.nytimes.com/2005/08/16/nyregion/16turkey.html.
2. Ibid.
3. Steven Waldman, "Beliefnet's Most Inspiring Person of 2005—Victoria Ruvolo," *Beliefnet*, accessed February 15, 2012, http://www.beliefnet.com/Inspiration/Most-Inspiring-Person-Of-The-Year/2005/Beliefnets-Most-Inspiring-Person-Of-2005-Victoria-Ruvolo.aspx?p=2.
4. Mead, "Deal in Turkey-Throwing Case."
5. Jonathan Lubliner, "Nobody Deserves a First Chance, That's Why They Get a Second (Yom Kippur 5770)," *Rabbi Jonathan Lubliner* (blog), January 2011, accessed February 15, 2012, http://rabbilubliner.files.wordpress.com/2011/01/nobody-deserves-a-first-chance-thats-why-they-get-a-second-yom-kippur-5770.pdf.
6. Jonathan Lemire, "Victoria Ruvolo, Who Was Hit by Turkey Nearly 6 Years Ago, Forgives Teens for Terrible Prank," *New York Daily News*, November 7, 2010, accessed February 15, 2012, http://articles.nydailynews.com/2010-11-07/local/27080547_1_victoria-ruvolo-ryan-cushing-forgives.
7. Lubliner, "Nobody Deserves a First Chance."
8. Lemire, "Victoria Ruvolo, Who Was Hit by Turkey."

Chapter 19
1. "Reinhold Niebuhr Quotes," Brainy Quote, accessed August 13, 2012, http://www.brainyquote.com/quotes/quotes/r/reinholdni121403.html.
2. "Woman Shows Incredible Mercy as Her Son's Killer Moves in Next Door," *Daily Mail*, June 8, 2011, accessed February 16, 2012, http://www.dailymail.co.uk/news/article-2000704/Woman-shows-incredible-mercy-sons-killer-moves-door.html.
3. Ibid.
4. Ibid.
5. Lewis B. Smedes, *Forgive & Forget: Healing the Hurts We Don't Deserve* (New York: HarperCollins, 1983), quoted in "50 Quotes on Forgiveness," ILoveULove, accessed February 16,

2012, http://www.iloveulove.com/wisdom/50quotes.htm.

6. Mary Johnson and Oshea Israel, interview by John Ortberg, "Forgiveness," Menlo Park, California, Presbyterian Church, July 10, 2011, accessed February 16, 2012, http://www.mppc .org/sites/default/files/transcripts/110710_jortberg.pdf.

7. Ibid.
8. Ibid.
9. Ibid.
10. Ibid.
11. Ibid.
12. Ibid.

13. Steve Hartman, "Love Thy Neighbor: Son's Killer Moves Next Door," *CBS Evening News,* June 7, 2011, accessed February 17, 2012, http://www.cbsnews.com/stories/2011/06/07 /eveningnews/main20069849.shtml.

14. Ibid.

15. Mary Johnson and Oshea Israel, "Forgiving Her Son's Killer: 'Not an Easy Thing,' " *StoryCorps,* National Public Radio, May 20, 2011, accessed February 16, 2012, http://www.npr.org /templates/transcript/transcript.php?storyId=136463363.

Chapter 20

1. Will King, "A Church From a Historically Anti-Semitic German Town Seeks Forgiveness in a March to Dachau," *Jerusalem Post,* May 30, 2007, accessed August 13, 2012, http://www.jpost .com/LandedPages/PrintArticle.aspx?id=63125.

2. Ibid.
3. Ibid.

4. Ellen G. White, *The Desire of Ages* (Mountain View, Calif.: Pacific Press®, 1940), 651.

5. "What Are Some Examples of Forgiveness Meditations?" *Sharecare,* accessed August 13, 2012, http://www.sharecare.com/question/what-some-examples-forgiveness-meditations.

Chapter 21

1. Ellen G. White, *The Desire of Ages,* 25.

2. Erwin Lutzer, quoted in Peter Kennedy, "Forgiven and Adopted," Sermon Illustrator, accessed February 27, 2012, http://www.sermonillustrator.org/illustrator/sermon13/forgiven_and _adopted.htm.

3. Maxwell Maltz, *Doctor Pygmalion* (New York: Thomas Y. Crowell Co., 1953), 133, 134.
4. Ibid., 135.
5. Ibid., 137.
6. Ibid., 139.
7. Ibid.
8. Ibid., 142.
9. Ibid., 141.

Chapter 22

1. Rick Reilly, "No Ordinary Joe," *Sports Illustrated,* July 2, 2003, accessed February 27, 2012, http://sportsillustrated.cnn.com/inside_game/rick_reilly/news/2003/07/01/reilly0707.

2. Ibid.

3. *Wikipedia* contributors, "Joe Delaney," *Wikipedia,* accessed August 13, 2012, http:// en.wikipedia.org/wiki/Joe_Delaney.

4. Glen Jacobs, quoted in "Joe Delaney Article. 37 Forever Props," Chiefs Planet, accessed February 12, 2012, http://www.chiefsplanet.com/BB/showthread.php?t=186016.

5. "Joe Delaney Article."
6. "Joe Delaney."
7. "Joe Delaney Article."
8. Ibid.
9. Reilly, "No Ordinary Joe."

Chapter 23

1.   Moody Adams, excerpts from *The* Titanic's *Last Hero* (Greenville, S.C.: Ambassador Publications, 1998); and "John Harper: True Hero on the *Titanic,*" *Blessed Quietness Journal,* accessed February 20, 2012, http://www.blessedquietness.com/journal/housechu/harper.htm. Used by permission of the author.

Chapter 24

1.   C. Douglas Sterner, "The Brotherhood of Soldiers at War: Richard Nott Antrim," Home of Heroes, accessed February 27, 2012, http://www.homeofheroes.com/brotherhood/antrim .html. The author provides the following special acknowledgment and sources: A very special "thank you" to Dick Antrim's daughter Judy Antrim Laylon for sharing her father's story with us and assisting in the preparation of this story. She has done so, not only out of a deep love and sense of respect for her father, but also a strong patriotic love for America. SOURCES: Judy Antrim Laylon; *Peru (Indiana) Republican,* Peru, Indiana; *Baxter Bulletin* (and specifically articles by Tom Dearmore); Edward F. Murphy, *Heroes of World War II* (New York: Presidio Press, 1990); the U.S. Naval Historical Center. Reprinted by permission of the author.

Chapter 25

1.   Sara Miles, *Take This Bread* (New York: Ballantine Books, 2007), xiii.
2.   Ellen G. White, *The Desire of Ages,* 661.

Conclusion

1.   Unless otherwise noted, all Scripture quotations are from the New Century Version of the Bible.
2.   Jerry D. Thomas, "Jesus Dies on the Cross," in *Messiah* (Nampa, Idaho: Pacific Press®, 2002). Used by permission.

❧

Karl Haffner

Got a story of self-sacrificing love? The author would love to hear it.
Contact him at:

Kettering SDA Church
3939 Stonebridge Road
Kettering, OH 45419

Fax: 937–298–7839
www.karlhaffner.com
✉ karlhaffner@gmail.com
🐦 Twitter: @karlhaffner
📘 Facebook: Karl Haffner

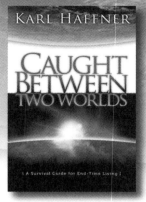

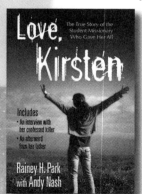